The Study Success Journal

Barbara Bassot

First published 2019 by
RED GLOBE PRESS

Red Globe Press in the UK is an imprint of Springer Nature Limited, registered in England, company number 785998, of 4 Crinan Street, London N1 9XW.

Red Globe Press® is a registered trademark in the United States, the United Kingdom, Europe and other countries.

ISBN 978–1–352–00549–3 paperback

This book is printed on paper suitable for recycling and made from fully managed and sustained forest sources. Logging, pulping and manufacturing processes are expected to conform to the environmental regulations of the country of origin.

A catalogue record for this book is available from the British Library.

A catalog record for this book is available from the Library of Congress.

Contents

Acknowledgements

I would like to express my sincere thanks to my family and friends for all their support in the process of bringing *The Study Success Journal* to fruition. In particular, I would like to thank Marc Bassot for his proof reading and constructive comments. I would also like to thank my Commissioning Editor, Helen Caunce, for her belief in the project, and to the publisher for being prepared to take a risk with another new publication.

Introduction

Welcome to *The Study Success Journal*. You are probably reading this because you are about to start or have recently started a course at university. You might be a first-year undergraduate, a student on a Foundation year, someone who has gone straight to university from school or college, or a mature student returning to study after some time away from education. Whatever your situation, *The Study Success Journal* is designed to help you to reflect on your learning (including your personal and academic development), in order to help you to gain the most from your studies. Studying at university can be described as a learning journey. Most journeys have ups and downs, highs and lows, and reaching a destination often requires patience and tenacity, especially if it is a fairly lengthy journey; your learning journey at university is no exception to this. Your journey has just begun and whilst it will undoubtedly present you with some challenges along the way, the destination of your graduation ceremony will be well worth it – here's to your future success!

Who this journal is for

The Study Success Journal is designed for all students who are new to higher education. It could also be useful if you are in your second year and want to review your progress to enhance it further. Starting a university course is exciting, but it also presents many challenges; in particular, it demands that you take responsibility for your own learning in order to become a more independent learner. You will need to do this quickly because it is surprising how easy it is to 'fall behind' in your studies. This book helps you to think through key aspects of your personal and academic development. Critical reflection lies at the heart of this process and the book's journal format helps you to engage with the necessary metaprocesses (thinking about thinking) to critically evaluate your learning and development. This puts you in charge of your studies, thereby enabling you to become more independent as a learner.

How to use this journal

The Study Success Journal is designed as a tool to help you reflect critically on your learning and development, thereby enabling you to take a deeper approach to it. Many university students are asked to write essays, projects and case studies as part of the assessment for particular modules, and some are also asked to write reflective pieces. This book shows you how to start writing reflectively and gives activities that help you to develop this vital skill. It also helps you to understand more about what critical reflection is so that you can assess how reflective your work is, and work to improve it where necessary. Many university students are asked to write in a critically reflective way. Whether you are asked to do this in a traditional essay format or writing a critical evaluation after carrying out an experiment or project, reflective work gains higher marks – something that all students want.

The role of writing in learning – writing for understanding

The overall aim of *The Study Success Journal* is to enable you to gain a deeper understanding of yourself and your studies through writing. I once attended a writers' seminar led by a professor who said, 'I have to write about things in order to understand them'. At the time this really opened my eyes, as I always thought that professors wrote a lot because they already understood a lot. His words turned this 'on its head' and showed me that the process of writing enables our knowledge and understanding to grow because it forces us to slow down and to take time to reflect. Unlike many of the books you will read at university, *The Study Success Journal* is one that you will be asked to write in – and I encourage you to do so!

What is critical reflection and why is it important?

Critical reflection is an important key to success in higher education and it is a skill. It can be defined as the process of critically evaluating experiences in order to learn from them, thereby increasing self-awareness. There are four key aspects of critical reflection that are worth looking at in some more detail.

1   Process – it takes time to work through and develop and is not something that happens automatically or in a rush. We should expect to devote some time to it if we want to improve in this area.

2   Evaluation – this involves examining our strengths and weaknesses, likes and dislikes. We need to be prepared to change if it is in our best interest, and most of us will need to work out some effective strategies to help us to achieve this.

3   Self-awareness – this means knowing ourselves well, which includes being honest about what we can do well and identifying those things we find difficult. Knowing what we are like as individuals and how we respond in situations is key in helping us to overcome such things as bad habits and procrastination.

4   Skill – this is something we do and that we can improve upon. Critical reflection is not something we can expect to do automatically, but it is a skill we can all learn, and we can all develop in this area.

Challenges of studying at university level

Prior to starting your university course, many of you will have received a relatively high level of support from your school or college, so the more independent nature of university study can be somewhat daunting. Even finding where you are meant to be at a given time can be a challenge in the first few weeks. Systems and procedures are new, and being part of a much larger community of learners, whilst also being exciting, can be a very different kind of experience from anything you have previously faced. Having opportunities to reflect on these changes is important for your ongoing development as you begin to adapt to the next phase of your academic life. You may find that you also need a guide to help you with some key terms that you may not have come across so far, and this book can help you to understand them.

Studying at university is not only an investment of time, it is a financial investment too and one that you will want to make the most of; in essence, becoming a university student means that you become a consumer of higher education. It is interesting to note that since the introduction of tuition fees there has been some growing evidence to show that students who take a consumerist approach to their education are likely to achieve less academically (Tomlinson, 2017). This is because as consumers we expect to receive; whether this is a good cup of coffee or a good lecture the same thing applies when we think about a consumerist approach. But succeeding at university is dependent on what we put in (hard work and effort) as well as what we receive. Good lectures, seminars, laboratories and libraries are undoubtedly important, but how you use them as a student is what will make a difference when it comes to your final degree classification.

Outline of contents

This book is organised in two parts. Part 1 is broken down into 10 themes. Each theme starts with a brief introduction and is followed by five pieces of content based on the theme, where some key theories are introduced in an accessible way. Each of these is followed by a practical activity and some space to write your reflections on it. Towards the end of each theme there is a larger activity to carry out and a case study of a student's experience. Both should give you some more 'food for thought'. Each theme finishes with a top tip to help you succeed in your studies.

Part 2 focuses on record keeping and your next steps. This includes notes pages for recording your marks and tables for your plans for the vacation period and for the coming academic year, including any module choices you might have to make. It will help you think about what you might do next and how you might prepare for your next year of study and for your future more broadly. It can also serve as a helpful record for the future.

Towards the end of the book there is a section with descriptions of important key terms, and things you need to know in order to succeed on your course.

I hope that you find *The Study Success Journal* helpful in your learning and academic development.

Barbara Bassot

> Education is not preparation for life. Education is life itself. – **John Dewey (1859–1952) American philosopher, psychologist, and educational reformer**

Part 1

Thème 1

Personal and academic development

This section will:

- ○ Help you to understand more about coping with change
- ○ Enable you to think about what motivates you in your studies
- ○ Help you to know where to go for support when you need it
- ○ Enable you to understand the importance of being an independent learner
- ○ Help you to think about your learning styles.

Education breeds confidence. Confidence breeds hope. Hope breeds peace. – **Confucius (551–479 BC) Chinese teacher, philosopher and politician**

Coping with change

Starting university is without doubt a major change in life, and the term transition is a more accurate way of summing up this experience. The word transition is used to describe a major change in someone's life from one state to another. It can include such things as bereavement, marriage, divorce and becoming a parent; you could also add going to university to this list. Starting university can mean a very different way of life from being at school or college (or working, if you are a mature student) and can also involve living in a different area with people who you have not met before. For international students it can mean a change of country and culture too. Transition is a process not an event, and it takes time to adjust to the changes that are taking place.

During any time of major change, it is common to experience a range of different emotions, including highs and lows, as you go through the transition process. Adams, Hayes and Hopson's (1976) work on transition has become seminal and their seven-stage model describes how many people think and feel during the process.

Stage 1 – Immobilisation. The process is very new and we can have a feeling of being overwhelmed by the enormity of the transition. We can find ourselves thinking things like 'will I ever be able to cope with all of this?'. We can 'freeze' and not know what to do next.

Stage 2 – Reaction of elation or despair. If the transition is seen as positive, we feel elated and might say things like 'this is all great!'. If we see it as negative we can have a sense of despair and think or say 'I wish I could go home'.

Stage 3 – Self-doubt or minimisation. As the impact of the transition becomes clearer, our elation turns to self-doubt and, as our feelings dip, we ask ourselves questions like 'am I really good enough to do a degree?'. Alternatively, our feelings of despair are minimised, and we tell ourselves things like 'maybe this won't be so bad after all'.

Stage 4 – Acceptance and letting go. This is about accepting that the change is happening and recognising that it won't go away. We start to look forward and begin to let go of the past.

Stage 5 – Testing. As we move on into the new situation, we begin to try out new ways of working and living.

Stage 6 – Search for meaning. This is a period of reflection when we contemplate what has happened and explore what the change means for us.

Stage 7 – Integration. We internalise the meaning from Stage 6 and accept the change as part of our everyday lives. The new state then becomes the norm.

These stages of transition show us that we often experience highs and lows over a period of time as we experience change, and that rushing in to make snap decisions (e.g. to change course or drop out because it's not what we expected) without discussing it with someone could be a mistake, as our feelings change over time. It is also useful to know about this for others too, so that we can offer support and encouragement to those around us when they need it.

Motivation

When starting something new it is good to understand what motivates us. Motivation is a difficult concept to define but includes the processes or factors that prompt us to act in certain ways. This can involve the identification of a particular need and how this might be satisfied, and sometimes involves the process of setting goals (see Theme 2.2). There are many theories that seek to explain what motivation is and how people are motivated, and understanding what motivates us can help us to succeed.

Different people are motivated by different things. Some are motivated by external (extrinsic) factors and others by things that are more internal (intrinsic). In relation to your time at university, here are some examples.

Extrinsic motivators

- Celebrating on graduation day
- Getting a good degree
- Gaining entry into the career I am hoping for
- The probability of earning a higher salary than I would without a degree
- Gaining respect and recognition from others.

Intrinsic motivators

- Doing something I really enjoy
- Developing my interests
- A sense of satisfaction
- A sense of pride and achievement
- A love of learning as much as I can about something.

Most of us are motivated by a mixture of extrinsic and intrinsic factors. However, it is worth remembering that there is growing evidence to suggest that those university students who take a consumerist approach to their learning tend to focus too much on extrinsic factors. These students might find themselves thinking things like 'I'm paying for this, so I expect better lectures' or even 'I'm paying for this, so I expect to get at least a 2:1'.

Such an approach takes the focus away from learning and means that someone's motivation can dwindle if they don't do as well as they hope. In these cases, they become very quick to blame other people for their lack of success instead of looking at their own contribution too. Succeeding at university involves taking ownership of your own learning, and having at least some focus on intrinsic factors will be important.

Motivation often changes over time; in the early days of being at university, meeting new people and making friends will be important motivators. But as time goes on, your motivation is likely to shift, for example towards reaching your longer-term goals. Reviewing what motivates you and reflecting on these changes as they happen can be a very helpful process. Whatever your situation is, it will be good to understand what motivates you at that time. For example, if things are tough (e.g. in the self-doubt phase of Adams et al.'s transition model in Theme 1.1) this can help you to build your resilience and keep your focus on things that will help you to succeed.

Try this   Make a list of what motivates you under the headings of extrinsics and intrinsics. What does this show you?

Getting the support you need

All of us need support at various times, and being at university is no different from other times (such as at school or college) when we need people around who can help us. It is important to understand that we need various kinds of support at different times, which means that no single person will always be able to support us. Being new to university life, it helps to know who to approach for help when you need it. Here are some examples.

Personal support

The early days of university can be exciting and daunting at the same time. Many universities have a personal tutor system and your personal tutor will often be your first point of contact for personal issues. Universities also have central services (such as counselling, accommodation and finance) that can offer more specialised support when needed.

Academic support

If you are unclear about your course or begin to have difficulties with academic work generally, support should be available by contacting the person who has the overall academic responsibility for your programme. They will often have the title of Programme Director or Course Director. It is always good to have a discussion with this person about any concerns you are having, particularly if you are thinking of changing your course or dropping out altogether. If you are having difficulties with a particular module, it is usually best to speak to the module tutor or lead module tutor. General academic support (such as how to read academic texts effectively and note taking) is often available centrally; this could be online via the portal or there may be dedicated study support staff in the library who you can ask. Library staff 'are used to people not being able to use libraries: if you need help, ask for it' (Cottrell, 2013:31).

Disability support

If you have any kind of disability, it will be good to make full use of the disability support that is available to you as this will help you to succeed in your studies. You may have made contact with the disability team before starting university, but if you haven't please be sure to do this as soon as you can. It can take a while for the appropriate support to be arranged, so the sooner you make contact the sooner they will be able to support you.

Many students experience difficulties at some point during their time at university, and it is important to remember that asking for help at these times is not a sign of weakness but a definite strength. Most universities have systems in place to help students who have genuine difficulties and if you don't seek help and support, staff will assume that everything is okay. If you need help, you will need to be proactive and make the first move, otherwise you could struggle on your own. Your fellow students can be a vital source of support too; this includes those you live with as well as those on your course. Joining some societies in freshers' week can make your pool of friends bigger. Remember that you can support them too when they need it.

Try this   Complete the table below, making a list of the people you will go to for academic and personal support. When might you need to contact them and why? How will you interact with them (e.g. face to face, via email)?

Name	Role	Support offered	Contact

Becoming an independent learner

Studying at university is different from other kinds of learning you might have taken part in so far because it usually demands that you take responsibility for your own learning, which leads to a much greater level of independence. In particular, there won't be anyone standing over you, checking what you have done and when. For many people this can be a great relief, whilst for others it can be a bit scary. Taking responsibility for your own learning will be important from the very beginning of your studies. Here are some important tips to help you take the first steps towards this.

○ Much of the basic information you need (e.g. your timetable) will probably be available online. Be sure to familiarise yourself with the university's system (sometimes called the portal) so you can find what you need quickly and easily.

○ During the early days, there will often be very useful induction sessions held to introduce you to key things related to your course, such as giving you an overview of the modules, the assessment requirements, the staff involved and so forth. Be sure to attend these as they also provide a great opportunity to meet your fellow students.

○ During the first few weeks it is also likely that more general induction sessions will be on offer, such as an introduction to the library facilities and an overview of study skills sessions. These can be very useful preparation for later in the term or semester, as you begin to prepare for your first assignments and/or examinations.

○ Be sure to find out when your assessed work is due and start your planning early (see Theme 2.4). Finding this out after a deadline has passed is far from ideal!

Knowing that most of the information you need to enable you to become an independent learner is available online is helpful, particularly because you can access it at any time and from any device that is connected to the internet. However, if you have problems accessing the portal, be sure to ask the relevant people as soon as you can, because it provides you with so much essential information. Universities usually have dedicated IT staff who specialise in this area who are available, sometimes 24 hours a day. Equally, if you search and can't find what you need, don't be afraid to ask. If you are someone whose IT skills are not as strong as they could be, people will usually be pleased to help, and your time at university could well offer a really good opportunity to do some of that IT training that you have been meaning to do for a while. Rest assured that if you take a proactive approach, you will soon feel in control of your studies.

Understanding your learning styles

Whatever subject you are studying, understanding your learning styles is an important aspect of helping you to succeed on your course. Honey and Mumford (2000) describe learning styles as learning habits that we have acquired over the years. They can give us vital clues about how we learn best and why we fail to learn in some circumstances, because, like all habits, some are good and some are bad. Understanding them will help us to gain more insights into our strengths and weaknesses and to see how we can develop.

Over a number of years Honey and Mumford (2000) carried out extensive work on the subject of learning styles and identified the following four distinct styles. Each style has its relative strengths; however, in addition they each have allowable weaknesses which become evident when we overdo our strengths.

○ **Activists** are doers who like to be involved in new experiences. They are open-minded and enthusiastic, enjoy getting on with things, and can achieve a lot in a short space of time. However, they tend to go into a situation 'feet first' without enough forethought, so they can be prone to making mistakes. If you have a strong Activist learning style you might find yourself feeling impatient and thinking things like 'when are things really going to get going?'

○ **Reflectors** are thinkers who like to stand back and look at a situation from different perspectives. They enjoy collecting information and thinking about things carefully before reaching any conclusions. They like observing other people and listening to their views before offering their own. However, they can be seen as slow and might panic in a crisis when they don't have enough time to think. A strong Reflector will often feel they would like more time to think and might say 'I wish I didn't have to do this yet'.

○ **Theorists** are analytical people who like to seek explanations for things. They often think problems through in a step by step way and can be perfectionists who like to fit things into a rational scheme or model. They have an ability to see things in a detached and objective way but at the same time can be seen as rather cold and calculating. They also find things difficult when there are no rational explanations. If you have a strong Theorist learning style you will love being in the library and might find yourself saying 'well let's just look at this in depth'.

○ **Pragmatists** are practical people who are keen to try out new ideas and prefer things that can be applied easily in practice. They enjoy problem solving and decision making but can become impatient when things do not appear to be working. They can also become cynical if they feel that an idea has been tried before and failed. People with a strong Pragmatist style take a very practical approach and might think 'well, that's ok in theory, but how will it work in practice?'

Most of us have a preference for more than one style. Strengths in all styles shows a strong, all round learner – so in order to gain most from your studies it is important to know your strengths and your least preferred styles; the latter will give you clear things to work on as you progress. Remember to look for the learning styles of others too, as this will help you to work well with your fellow students.

Try this

Think about your learning styles (Honey and Mumford, 2000). Which are your preferred styles? Which ones do you feel you need to develop?

Activity As you are near the beginning of your studies, now is a good time to think about what you hope to gain from your time at university. In his work *The 7 Habits of Highly Effective People*, Covey (2004:95) says that we should 'begin with the end in mind' (Habit 2). He argues that everything is created twice – first in our minds and then in what we do in our everyday lives. We need to look ahead and to have a personal vision for the future. Interestingly, he also says that if we do not have a vision of our own, we might live lives where the vision and priorities of others are more important than our own.

So, imagine it is your graduation day and think about the following questions:

○ Who will be at your graduation?
○ What classification of degree would you like to receive?
○ What might you be doing next?

Case study: New beginnings

Charlie has just started his course at university and is beginning to feel a bit lost. Initially he was very excited, but is now a bit overwhelmed by all the new information he needs to take in. He is getting used to using the online student virtual learning environment (VLE, e.g. Blackboard, Moodle) but is worried about missing things that are important.

At an induction session Charlie meets his personal tutor, and he decides to email her afterwards with a couple of queries. Charlie's tutor replies and suggests that he attends her weekly 'clinic' session, which is being held in her office later that afternoon. Charlie goes along and his tutor responds to his queries and takes him through some useful information to help him to 'find his feet' more quickly. In particular she advises him where to go to for help with the online student portal and gives him lots of reassurance. She encourages him to keep in contact by email to ask any questions he feels he needs to ask. She explains that she will be available each week at the same time to speak to any student who has a concern about their studies. Charlie also meets some more of the students on his course at the 'clinic' and they go for coffee afterwards to share some tips.

Top tip The first week – blink and you'll miss it!

The first week at university passes by very quickly, and it is surprising how easy it is to get behind without even realising it. With so much going on in your early days of being at university, it is difficult to take everything in. Making new friends, socialising and getting to know where things are will all be very important, but you will also want to make the most of things that are offered to help you to make a good start to your academic studies. Theme 1.4 gives you some ideas of key events to look out for, so make sure you make a note to attend these. Missing these vital sessions can 'put you on the back foot' so you don't know what to expect. Even after just a few weeks you can then feel that you are behind, and it can be very difficult to catch up as the end of the first term or semester quickly approaches. Whilst catching up can be difficult, remember that most things will be on your VLE and there will always be people you can ask to help you. If you find yourself in this position, be proactive, you will recover, and it will be worth it!

Time management and taking charge of your studies

This section will:

- Introduce you to a model for successful study
- Help you to assess your priorities and set some goals
- Help you to think about how best to keep your focus and concentration
- Enable you to plan for important deadlines and beat procrastination
- Help you to make sure you get some quality time for yourself.

Better three hours too soon than a minute too late. – **William Shakespeare (1564–1616) English poet, playwright and actor**

A model for successful study

In the early days of your course it can be very useful to start to get a clear picture of what the coming semester or term will involve. The phrase 'forewarned is forearmed' is important here; knowing what to expect is a great coping mechanism and will help you to 'find your feet'. Here is a simple model, OPI, that will help you to find a focus and begin to plan ahead.

Overview (O) – getting a clear overview is an important first step in being able to see what is coming up. Look at your timetable to find out which modules you are studying in your first semester or term. Now look at the module outlines to see what they entail; you will find these amongst some important documents (e.g. your Programme Handbook) on your VLE. Be sure to look at the suggested reading lists too.

Plan (P) – now start planning your time. This is as basic as making sure that all your lectures, seminars and tutorials are in your diary or calendar. If you know that you can be forgetful at times (and let's face it, we can all be like that), be sure to set alerts to remind you. You will need to allow plenty of time for assignment preparation, as the academic work will be more challenging. You will also need to include the deadline dates for the submission of all your assessed work. Believe me, missing one of these is not a good option!

Implement (I) – now it's time to get on and do things. It is always very easy to procrastinate and to put things off. University semesters and terms are notoriously short. It might be difficult to believe this in the early days, but before you know it you will be heading for the next vacation. If you don't implement your plan, very quickly you can become 'unstuck' and panic as deadlines begin to loom large. Falling behind can be very stressful, so keeping to your plan will help you to avoid this (Bedford and Wilson, 2013).

Make a list of things that you need to do this semester or term under the headings of OPI.

Overview (including the modules you are studying, main tasks and deadline dates)

Plan (including dates and times of lectures, seminars, tutorials)

Implement (your plans for achieving the above)

Goal setting and prioritising

When you have an overview of the work you will be doing in the coming semester, term or academic year, you will be in a good position to set some goals. Goal setting is seen to be very important in many different areas of life, and it is important that the goals you set for yourself are challenging but also achievable. Locke and Latham (1990) argue that if we set ourselves challenging goals, we will work hard to achieve them. Once we have achieved our goals, we are in a good position to set some more. This cycle, sometimes called the high-performance cycle, is often depicted as an upward moving spiral. It is good to know that as well as upward spirals, there are downward ones too. This means that if we set goals that are too difficult, we will get discouraged when we can't achieve them, and the cycle will move downwards instead of up.

Setting realistic and achievable goals is always difficult, especially if you haven't done it before and if you are in a new or different situation. If in doubt, it is usually best to start by setting yourself a goal you know you can achieve. You will then get the satisfaction of achieving it; if it's too easy, you can always set a more challenging one next time. Goal setting should get easier the more you do it and the more experience you have.

Once you have a clear picture of what lies ahead by following the OPI process, and have set some goals, you will be in a good position to start to list the things that you need to do to succeed. Making lists can help most people for the following reasons.

○ You are less likely to forget things.
○ You don't have to waste valuable time trying to remember what you need to do, you can just get on and do it.
○ It gives you some 'head space' and reduces your levels of stress.
○ You can get some satisfaction by crossing things off your list.
○ It helps you to stay focused.

Where you keep your list really doesn't matter but be sure to put it somewhere accessible where you won't lose it easily. This might be on your phone or tablet or in a notebook. As your list becomes out of date (hopefully because you have completed most things but also because you will need to add new tasks) you will need to make a new one.

But making lists is only the first step; now you need to prioritise the items on your list, placing them in order of importance and considering their level of urgency. Urgent tasks are things we need to do soon (e.g. when a deadline is looming); important tasks may not need to be done straight away but will often help us to reach our long term goals (such as getting the degree classification we want). Over time if tasks are left, they become increasingly more urgent. In most cases, top of your list will be things that you know you need to do now or very soon, followed by things that you know can be done later.

Try this
Now set yourself three goals for this semester or term that are related to your studies; try to make sure they are achievable. Then make a list of things that you need to do to achieve your goals and list them in order of priority.

Staying focused and keeping your concentration

Many students say they find it difficult to stay focused and concentrate on their work, even when they are doing things that they enjoy. Academic reading can be particularly challenging, unlike your favourite book that you could easily read from start to finish. It is easy to start reading, and then before you know it, your mind drifts off, you get to the end of the page and you can't remember what you've read. Then you start all over again. It is worth knowing that most of us can concentrate well for 30–45 minutes, so we need regular breaks.

Keeping your focus and concentration is a skill, and here are some tips that might help you.

- Find a place to study where you will be comfortable and not be disturbed. This could be in your room, in the library, your faculty, or a quiet corner in the coffee shop.
- Turn off your phone and email.
- Take regular breaks. During your breaks, do something different like going for a short walk, making a drink or a having snack.
- Listen to music if it helps. If you like silence and can't find any (this can be especially difficult in student accommodation), listen to some 'white noise' on your headphones and you will soon have the silence you long for.
- When you know you have something difficult to read or write, break it down into sections and do them one at a time.
- Vary your study activities, for example do some reading, followed by some online research then going to the library to find some more resources.
- Eat well and stay hydrated.
- Get plenty of sleep; everything is more difficult when you are tired.

○ Be sure to reward yourself when you keep to your plans. This will give you something to look forward to and will make you feel like you are making progress.

○ Find a study group and encourage one another (see Theme 8.1).

Remember that all of these things can help, but you need to find what works for you. So be prepared to give something a try – if it works, great, but if it doesn't, don't be afraid to move on to something else that might.

Managing deadlines and beating procrastination

Being a university student requires a lot of independent learning. Until now you may well have had people to remind you about key things you need to do and by when; in particular the work you need to submit. This is now something that you need to manage for yourself. Now that you have an overview of the work ahead, you will need to manage your time in more detail to make sure that you meet your deadlines. So how can you do this? You have already made a start by using the OPI model, but now you need to move on to the next step.

Many deadlines will seem a long way away to start with (e.g. the end of the term or semester) and it is easy to be fooled into thinking that you can work on everything later because you have plenty of time. Putting things off, or procrastination, is often called 'the thief of time'. By delaying everything, you lose the time you have; or more accurately, the time you have now is stolen from you by failing to take any action. There are many different ways we can procrastinate, and some are more obvious than others. We have all given in to more tempting ways of spending our time, for example, playing our favourite sport, going to a gig or simply spending time with friends. By contrast we can feel virtuous about doing a large amount of academic reading, but if this is stopping us from writing and assignment, this can be procrastination too. If you have a strong Theorist learning style (see Theme 1.5) you will probably always feel that you need to read more, and it will be important to know when to stop!

As Smale and Fowlie (2009: 81) point out, 'Time ... is the only resource which we all have equally, and it is the most valuable resource we have. Once used, it has gone forever'. So, overcoming procrastination is a vital skill to learn and can be achieved by using the 'salami method'. As we know, a salami is a large sausage that we usually eat in thin slices. Even those of us who love salami would be hard pressed to eat a whole one, and if we did, it would probably play havoc with our digestive system! Large tasks, such as producing a good piece of academic work, cannot usually be achieved in one go, and it is important to break things down into smaller parts. Using the salami method to do this kind of detailed planning can help you to start working on a task in good time, and, as you take small steps towards the deadline, you will feel you are making progress. This will help you to reduce your stress levels and prevent you from panicking.

Try this   Now think about your first deadline for a piece of assessed work and how you will work towards it. Count the number of weeks between now and the deadline. Then make a provisional weekly plan of what you think you need to do and by when. Remember to include attending lectures, seminars and tutorials, independent reading, time for writing, revision or preparation, making corrections, and proof reading. Your plan should be flexible, so be sure to allow plenty of time so you can make changes at a later date if you need to do so.

If you find this difficult (and many students do), try starting at the end and working backwards. Here is a general example, assuming you have 10 weeks to complete an assignment. Remember that you will often need to work on more than one piece of work at a time.

Week 10 – submit work.

Week 9 – final proof reading and corrections.

Week 8 – complete second draft.

Week 7 – check through first draft and work on second draft.

Week 6 – complete first draft.

Week 5 – continue relevant reading and note taking. Continue work on first draft. Go through lecture notes.

Week 4 – continue relevant reading and note taking. Start work on first draft and attend tutorial. Go through lecture notes.

Week 3 – continue relevant reading and note taking. Start to organise notes in line with your assignment plan. Go through lecture notes.

Week 2 – make an assignment plan and book a tutorial or session with support team if needed. Continue relevant reading and note taking. Go through lecture notes.

Week 1 – read assignment brief thoroughly and ask module tutor for clarity if needed. Start relevant reading and note taking. Go through lecture notes.

Time for yourself

Having some time for yourself is important on a number of levels. Here are some examples and you may well be able to think of more.

○ Being at university is a great opportunity to meet new people. Especially if you are studying away from home, it can be a unique experience where you live alongside many of your friends and can see them more or less whenever you want; it is good to enjoy this opportunity.

○ Many students who leave home can feel lonely at times. Some experience this in the early weeks and for others it can be a bit later as things start to settle down. Planning a nice activity (e.g. watching your favourite film or spending time with old friends and family) can really help at those times.

○ Everyone needs to relax. If we work all the time, we can quickly become exhausted and our stress levels can rise (see Theme 9.5).

○ Being at university is a great opportunity to become involved in things outside your course, such as clubs and societies that can help you to continue with some of your interests (e.g. sport, music, drama) and to develop some new ones. All of this will look good on your future CV.

○ Having a supportive mentor can really help you to manage your life and studies, especially when things are very new. Many universities have peer mentoring programmes that link a first-year student with a student in the year above and it is well worth considering signing up for this. Next year you could do this for a new student – another great thing to have to add to your CV!

Activity Having completed this section, it is now a good time to devise a study plan for the term or semester. Here are some ideas of what to include, and you may be able to think of more. Feel free to do this in whatever way suits you (e.g. a list, table, spreadsheet, calendar, timelines).

○ Modules
○ Pieces of assessed work and submission dates
○ Examinations
○ Preliminary work needed (e.g. reading, note taking, tutorial with module leader, first draft, corrections, final draft)
○ Other activities outside course
○ Visiting friends and family
○ Volunteering
○ Peer mentoring
○ Paid work

Case study: A mistake you only make once

Michael has now finished his first term at university and is at home enjoying his Christmas break. The term has gone quickly, and he has really enjoyed everything about being at university. He knows that he has some exams to sit before the start of the second semester and decides to look on the VLE to get some more detail. To his horror he finds that he should have submitted a piece of course work before the Christmas holiday and the deadline was two weeks ago. Michael panics and discusses this with his mum when she gets home from work. He admits to her that he did not know about the work because he has not been attending lectures. Michael decides to contact the module tutor by email.

Michael's tutor is understanding and encourages him to complete the work. The tutor explains that because he has missed the deadline by more than a week, he will be awarded a mark of 0% but that he will have the opportunity to re-submit the work. However, his mark for the work will then be capped at 40%. Michael is relieved, but also 'kicking himself' and decides to complete the work during the Christmas break. He emails it to the module tutor with an apology and an explanation of what has happened.

When he gets back to university, the module tutor asks to see him. He accepts Michael's apology and thanks him for being conscientious when he realised his mistake. He explains that he can only give Michael a mark of 40% because of the circumstances but says that he would have achieved 65% if the work had been submitted on time. Michael is pleased and knows that this is a mistake he will not make again.

Top tip — Managing multiple deadlines

One of the most difficult things about being at university is managing multiple assessment deadlines. Often you will be asked to submit more than one piece of work on a particular date; this makes the need for planning even more important. If you tend to leave things until the last minute, you could easily find yourself with the supermarket shopping experience of 'squashed bread'; as your shopping continues moving on the conveyor belt towards the till, your bread literally gets squashed! In the same way, as you move towards your assessment deadline, you begin to feel 'squashed' by the pressure of all the work you need to complete.

So how can you avoid this? Detailed planning is key here and having that clear overview as presented in the OPI model (see Theme 2.1) is vital. You may well need to have two or more plans (like the one in Theme 2.4) running side by side. This is difficult and many students say they find it easiest to work on one piece of work at a time rather than more than one. But if you only work on one piece at a time, you might well run out of time for the rest and submit work that you are not happy with.

So, what can you do? Here are some tips to help you.

○ When you devise your plan, mark out some specific time for each piece of work you need to complete.

○ Think about the balance of time; you will find some work more difficult than others, so be sure to allow more time for this.

○ Don't leave all the difficult work until the end; it works better to do at least some of the difficult things early, as this will give you time to do more reading or to get some support if you need it.

○ Use Turnitin as a time management tool – if you submit your work through Turnitin before the deadline date and then find that you have some time to make some changes to it, you can submit your work again and Turnitin will 'overwrite' it. This also means that if time runs out on you, you have submitted something by the deadline and won't be penalised for late submission.

Many students find managing multiple deadlines difficult, so why not discuss it with other students on your course; you might be able to give and pick up some useful tips.

Critical thinking

This section will:

- ○ Introduce you to the concepts of critical thinking and critical reasoning
- ○ Explain the difference between description and analysis
- ○ Examine the skill of evaluation
- ○ Explore the difference between critique and criticism
- ○ Demonstrate the need to present a balanced argument.

> Education is not the learning of facts, but training the mind to think. – **Albert Einstein (1879–1955) German physicist**

What is critical thinking?

Critical thinking means the ability to think purposefully and clearly about any subject, in order to evaluate it; this enables some conclusions to be reached that can be justified with robust evidence. Beginning your studies at university means that critical thinking is a process that you need to engage with, and it is a skill you can learn and develop. It is often referred to as critical reasoning.

Even if you would already describe yourself as a critical thinker, you will still need to become stronger in this area as your studies progress. The critical thinking process involves being prepared to question everything, even things you have previously accepted at 'face value' (Eales-Reynolds, Judge, McCreery and Jones, 2013). By doing this you examine ideas and issues at a deeper level, so that you can then begin to frame your arguments in a convincing way. Depending on your specific area of study, getting beneath the surface means that there is rarely a single correct answer. So far in your studies you might have become used to 'giving' the teacher or tutor what they want through description. Now is the time to move on and to start questioning everything, weighing one argument against another (or in some cases several arguments) to reach a balanced conclusion.

Putting this into practice in the early weeks of your studies can be difficult, especially if you are not used to it. One helpful starting point is to devise questions that you can pose when you are reading or going over your notes from lectures or seminars. Here are some examples, and once you get going you will probably be able to think of more for yourself.

- What are the main points being discussed?
- What are the arguments being presented (e.g. for and against)?
- How strong are the arguments that are being made? Examine the evidence being presented; how convincing is it? In light of this, give it a score on a scale where 1 = weak, 5 = average and 10 = strong or convincing.
- What am I learning that is building on what I know already?
- What am I learning that is new?

Questioning everything might seem strange at first because for many students, education so far has been about being given answers. When you embrace a critical approach through questioning and analysis, your thinking will become deeper; this will give you a firm foundation for success in your studies at university.

What is the difference between description and analysis?

Critical thinking also involves analysis; this means being ready to examine something in detail to understand its component parts. This is different from a detailed description of something. For example, a detailed description of the best holiday I have ever had will include where I went, how I travelled there and what I did each day. An analysis of it goes further to examine such things as why I chose to go to that particular place, what I enjoyed so much about it and why.

Many students have difficulty in understanding the difference between description and analysis. They know that they need to make their work analytical but can struggle to get beyond merely describing what they have read or heard. The table below highlights some of the differences between description and analysis.

Description	Analysis
States what has happened	Explains what has happened and gives some of the reasons why and/or how
States what something is like	Explores the relative strengths and weaknesses of something
States how to do something	Considers a range of different ways something could be done
Outlines a theory	Identifies strengths, weaknesses and gaps in a theory
Explains several theories	Compares and contrasts theories
Explains how something works	Considers why something works and why it might not in certain situations
Lists component parts	Evaluates different parts one against the other

To succeed at university, you will need to focus on analysis rather than description, so concentrating on the right-hand side of the table above will be important. Some tutors will probably say that some description is fine because you need to introduce a topic to then be able to analyse it. Others will say that words used on description are words lost from analysis.

Understandably, it is very confusing when tutors say different things; there are two important points here.

1   Just describing something does not show that you have understood it. At best it shows that you can paraphrase from something published (e.g. a book, article) and at worst that you can copy. Please don't go there (see Theme 7.1)! Analysing something as shown in the table above shows your knowledge and understanding.

2   Annoying as it is, tutors will vary in their advice. If you are in doubt about how much description to include, remember to ask the tutor who will be marking your work; and don't be surprised when you get different responses from different tutors.

Try this   Use the space below to describe your week. Simply state what you did and when. Then write an analysis of it and think about the following questions.

○ What did you enjoy and why?
○ What did you not enjoy and why not?
○ Consider your options for next week.
○ Discuss what you want to focus on and why.

Now compare what you have written – a simple description and a more detailed analysis.

What does the term evaluation mean?

The term evaluation is often used in relation to academic writing and discussion, so it is important to understand what it means. Evaluation often follows analysis and involves assessing the value or merit of something, and then making some kind of judgement about it. However, all evaluation needs to be defendable; in other words, you will always need to present strong evidence to show how you have reached your conclusions. Here are some pointers to help you to differentiate between what constitutes strong and weak evaluation.

Strong evaluation is:

○ Systematic – done in a clear and logical way, where points follow on one from the other
○ Thorough – does not miss anything or have any obvious gaps
○ Detailed – done fully and comprehensively
○ Carefully considered – well thought through
○ Balanced – fair, unbiased and considers all sides
○ Thought provoking – interesting and prompts new ideas
○ Based on evidence – informed by research, practice or literature
○ Justifiable – defendable.

Weak evaluation is:

○ Haphazard – random, disorganised and unplanned
○ Shallow – lacking in depth and simplistic
○ General – not detailed and only includes basic points
○ Not thought through – rushed and jumps to conclusions
○ One sided – biased and prejudiced
○ Superficial – flimsy and can easily be rejected
○ Based on opinion only – too subjective
○ Unjustifiable – unable to stand up to critique.

As part of the process of evaluation you will need to reach some conclusions, so the final points in each of the lists above are particularly important. 'Sitting on the fence' is usually not a good option, as doing this means that your conclusions are likely to appear weak. You need to be able to put your own views across, but you need to be able to justify them. At some point in any evaluation you will need to be clear about the reasons for your decisions or statements, and being able to justify them will always make your evaluation stronger.

What is the difference between critique and criticism?

To develop skills of critical thinking, it is important to understand the difference between critique and criticism. The word critical is often seen as a negative one. The phrase 'he or she is very critical' is likely to make you think of someone who is always quick to point out the bad side of something, or what went wrong. Critical thinking involves critique and is linked with evaluation. The table below highlights some of the differences between critique and criticism.

Criticism	Critique
Focuses on negatives	Focuses on positives, negatives and what can be improved
Discusses weaknesses	Discusses strengths, weaknesses and areas for development
Finds faults and flaws	Finds things that work well, things that could work better and also gaps or things that might have been overlooked
Presents a one-sided argument	Presents a balanced argument
Is often biased	Is carefully judged
Is destructive	Is constructive
Condemns	Questions

It is also important to remember that good critique does not only focus on the positives. This can be difficult when you are considering theory that might be seen as seminal in your particular area. A seminal theory is one that has stood the test of time and remained relevant and helpful even though it was probably written a long time ago. A good example of a seminal theory is Maslow's hierarchy of need; first written in 1943, it is still seen as valuable and relevant and is often referred to today. Theories like this can sometimes be seen as being beyond critique, so you might find yourself thinking 'how can I critique Maslow when his work is so widely accepted?' Even so it is important to do so. And don't forget, he has had his critics in the past and you can always look at what they have said when formulating your own critique.

Try this

Think of something you have done recently. This could be something you have read, a film you have seen, a concert or event that you have attended. Now write a critique of it, focusing on the points made on the right-hand side of the table above.

Presenting a balanced argument

Making a strong academic argument involves presenting both sides in a balanced way. When we read something we like, and that we agree with, it can be very difficult to critique it. The difficulty here is if we only present positives, our argument will probably be weak and one-sided. The same applies if we read something we disagree with; in this particular case our work is likely to be too negative and we can struggle to present any positives. When we present both sides of an argument, our work will usually be more robust and persuasive; as Metcalfe (2006:16) points out, 'After identifying the argument in a passage, the next task of the critique is to reflect on the counter argument.'

Presenting a balanced argument can be difficult and here are some suggestions to help you to achieve this.

○ You need to justify everything you are saying, so after each point ask yourself the question 'why?' If you cannot answer this question you probably need to add more detail to strengthen your argument.

○ Often you will also need to add the question 'says who?' Again, this ensures that you are justifying your point with reference to theory and research; otherwise your point is an assertion at best and your opinion at worst.

○ Be sure to present both sides of the argument in relatively equal detail. Your argument will be weak if you present one side strongly and skim over the other. For example, if you give two reasons for carrying out experiments on animals and 10 reasons for not doing this, your argument will be unbalanced.

○ In many instances your work will be more analytical if you present the relative strengths and weaknesses side by side rather than all the strengths followed by all the weaknesses. This will prevent your work from appearing repetitive and will enable you to have an ongoing debate with the reader. For example, if you present all the benefits of expanding genetic research followed by the drawbacks, you will inevitably find that you repeat yourself and the reader might need to refer back to what you wrote earlier.

This might sound strange, but whether or not you agree with the points you are making is not always the most important thing. It is the strength of your points and the evidence you present that often matters more. Remember, strong arguments are always justified by evidence from theory and research.

Try this We all know that the sky is blue, and the grass is green. But let's imagine we want to argue the opposite – how would we do this and what would our evidence be? What evidence will you need to present? Feel free to use your imagination here. Remember, on one level it doesn't matter if you really think the sky is blue and the grass is green; you can argue the opposite, but it must be convincing and supported with clear evidence.

Activity Presenting an argument is often easier if the topic is contentious; i.e. something that people often disagree about and where there is no clear 'correct' answer or view. Try thinking about an area like this (e.g. abortion, euthanasia, using animals in the advancement of medical research). Use the table below to write down the arguments for and against.

Title of topic area	
Pros	Cons

Case study: Getting lower marks than before

Casey has settled in well at university and has submitted her first pieces of academic work. She feels pleased with what she has done but is disappointed with the marks she has received, because they are much lower than the marks she used to get at college. So, she decides to book an appointment with the learning support team to discuss how she might improve. At her appointment Casey and the tutor go through some of the feedback she has received, and they find a common theme is that her work is too descriptive.

Casey is confused by this because at college she was always told that she needed to describe theory to show her understanding of it. The tutor explains that to gain higher marks she now needs to focus more on analysis and less on description. She asks Casey to go through her work and highlight all those parts that are descriptive and to book another appointment so they can go through things again.

Casey does this and is surprised to find that she highlights almost half of her work. She quickly realises that in many parts her arguments are weak (if there are any there at all) and that she needs to write in a different way. When she meets with the tutor again they review her work and discuss how she can make it more analytical. In particular the tutor encourages her to look at key text books related to her course and to examine how the authors present both sides of their arguments and to use some of the online resources available through the VLE. Casey agrees to do this and welcomes the support of the tutor in this vital area of her academic development.

Top tip   **You are not alone!**

Many of the ideas introduced in this theme can be challenging and difficult to grasp. Critical thinking is an abstract concept, which makes it difficult to identify and understand. At times it might seem that everyone around you understands everything, and you are the only one who doesn't. As a result, you might start to feel inadequate and 'out of your depth'. The meaning of terms like 'theory' and 'research' might seem obvious, but many students would not be able to explain what they mean if they were asked.

So, if you find yourself in this situation, what should you do?

○ Always talk to someone – often it is easier to ask a fellow student in your group first rather than a lecturer or tutor.

○ Ask individually – rather than asking in front of the whole group, ask the tutor or lecturer at the end of the session.

○ Do some research of your own and then ask – looking at reliable internet sources (e.g. those ending in .ac.uk) first will help.

○ Don't put it off – it's always easier to do this early on rather than leaving it.

As a result, you will probably find that you are not the only one who doesn't understand everything.

Critical reading

This section will:

○ Help you to understand the term critical reading

○ Help you to find and use reliable resources

○ Enable you to think about a range of reading skills that you will need while at university

○ Help you to find what you need in books and other resources

○ Show you how to make useful notes.

> Reading is to the mind what exercise is to the body. – **Joseph Addison (1672–1719) English essayist, poet, playwright, politician and classical scholar**

Theme 4.1 What is critical reading?

Critical reading is an important skill and is usually a precursor to critical writing (see Theme 5). Like critical thinking, to read critically you need to be prepared to delve deeper and avoid simply accepting things at face value. It involves examining the arguments or evidence being presented by the author, thinking about what has influenced them and the interpretations they might have made, and deciding how far you are prepared to accept their conclusions. Remember too that it means looking at the positives and strengths of their work as well as the weaknesses, limitations and gaps.

In most academic areas (even scientific ones), to read critically you need to

○ Consider the work as the author's argument only, rather than absolute truth. Any theory is one person's explanation of something (or it might of course have been written by two or three people, or even a group), and is likely to be only one explanation of several or, in some cases, many.

○ Find out more about the author and think about what might have influenced their work. An internet search is useful here.

○ Consider the context of the work, who it was written for and how this might be relevant.

○ Think about when the work was written. If it was written some time ago, is it dated or seminal?

○ Be prepared to set your own opinions or pre-judgements to one side.

○ Enter into an academic debate where you look for as many different positions on the work as you can find.

○ Keep an open mind and be prepared to disagree with your initial thoughts, and even to prove yourself wrong.

○ Make your own evaluation.

○ Seek out robust evidence.

○ Identify the limitations in the work.

Remember that critical reading can be particularly difficult if you agree with what has been written, but even so, you still need to engage with it. Looking for the author's critics and reading their work can usually help with this. In addition, always be sure to read the latest edition of the author's work if you can. Don't be surprised when an author's position on something changes over time; they are learning too and their work is developing. Discussing some of the detail of these changes in a piece of written work can be insightful and shows that you have done some research. Reading the latest version of an author's work will also mean that your reference list (see Theme 7) is up to date.

Try this   Now read a chapter from one of the books on your reading
list and write some notes under the following questions.

○ What is your initial impression of the work?

○ When was the work written?

○ Is this the latest version of their work?

○ Is the work dated or seminal?

○ Make a list of the arguments the author is making. Then note down the
evidence they use to support each one. How strong do you feel their
arguments are?

○ Where are the weaknesses in their arguments?

○ Are there any gaps or things that they don't seem to consider?

○ Look back at what you have written under the first point above. Has your
view changed? If so, how and if not, why not?

○ Has answering the subsequent questions caused you to change your
opinion?

Finding and using reliable resources

During your studies it will be important to find and use reliable resources. It is always important to remember that not all resources are good resources, and as Cottrell (2013:162) points out, 'Only a small proportion of the vast amount of information available in print and online will be suitable for academic assignments'. This means you need to become skilled at knowing which resources to use and which to leave to one side. Here are some tips to help you.

- Be sure to have a browse round the library in the early days of your studies. University libraries are big and you will need to find the sections of it that are most appropriate for your course. Then you will be able to find them quickly when you need to do so later on.

- Your online library catalogue is a vital resource and getting to grips with it early on in your studies will be extremely helpful. Many libraries run sessions and workshops to help you with this; if so, do book a place on one of them and start using it to make it work for you.

- The library staff are often a very helpful resource too. If you are struggling to find a particular resource, are not sure about where to look, or are even unsure about what you are looking for, do ask one of the library staff. Some university libraries have subject specific librarians. These people specialise in knowing about and finding resources in particular academic areas. Find out if your university has them, and if they do, who the librarian is for your area of study. They will be a good person to get to know, and you will probably find that like most library staff, they will be very willing to help, especially if you are pleasant and polite!

- We all know that the internet is a wonderful thing, but there are some words of caution here regarding its use. Always use a reputable search engine that focuses on scholarly work. When browsing on websites, again be sure to use ones that are robust (e.g. those published by a university or a scientific or professional body).

- Remember to use your module reading lists as a starting point. Many of these publications will have reference lists within them which can help you to find other relevant publications.

For many university students money is tight, so it is well worth borrowing books first before buying them. This way you can probably gauge how much you will use a particular book and decide later whether or not you want to buy it. Remember too that many books are available second hand, either through your university bookshop or online. Borrowing key texts from the library will be fine, until the book you really need isn't available and you have to wait for it to be recalled. Even worse is having the book you really need with an important deadline looming, and having to return it because another student has requested it.

Reading skills

Studying at university inevitably involves doing a lot of reading. In the early days it is easy to think that when you are asked to read something that you must read every word. Realistically this will not be possible, or even desirable. In addition, tutors will soon begin to speak about additional reading or 'reading around' a subject or topic too, so it is good to understand the different kinds of reading skills you will need. Here are some of them, with examples of when you might need to use them.

- Detailed reading – this is where you read something word for word and line by line. You will need to do this with key texts (or parts of them) to focus on the detail of what is being discussed.
- Close reading – this is where you focus on a particularly important paragraph or even a key sentence to 'unpick' what it says. This might involve identifying certain words that the author uses for emphasis and highlighting what they mean.
- Scanning – this is where you read to find things that you need (e.g. for a seminar or assignment). This means looking for key words and phrases, focusing on these and skipping over the rest. One good way to approach this is to read the first sentence of each paragraph.
- Skimming – this involves reading something quickly to get an overview of what a book or a chapter is saying. You may find that you want to go back later and read parts of it more closely.
- Reading for rejection – this is like skim reading, but here you read something 'just in case' it might be valuable and add something to what you have read already. You can do this to check that there is nothing more that has been written on a topic that is new to you. Some students find it difficult to know when to stop reading; being aware of when you begin to feel that you have read similar things before is often an indicator of when to stop.

One key point to remember is that all the reading you do needs to be active reading; this is where you read for a purpose. Many students waste lots of time by reading randomly, without knowing why they are reading what they are reading. The first important step in making your reading count is to ask yourself the question 'why am I reading this?'. You might then set yourself some goals to keep you focused and to help your level of concentration. It will be good to go back to these if (or more likely when) you find your mind wandering. In addition, it will be good to use the points above to check whether or not you are reading in the most effective way. For example, if you decide you need to read something in a detailed way only to find that the work doesn't contain what you thought it would, you can feel free to skim read it instead, or even not to read it at all. Don't be afraid to make some adjustments, as this will ensure that you use the time you have to best effect. Don't forget too that when concentrating becomes difficult it might be time to take a break (see Theme 2.3).

Theme 4.4 Finding what you need in books and resources

Sometimes thinking about what you need to read and the amount of information available can be daunting and even overwhelming. At times like this, as well as understanding where to look for what you need, it is also vital to know how to find the relevant parts in the sources you have identified. This can help to save you lots of time, and here are some suggestions that should help.

○ Books – many academic books contain two vital tools to help you to navigate your way through the text. First, the contents page; this breaks the book down into chapters, often with sub sections. This can help to guide you to the most relevant parts to read. Second, the index; this often includes topic areas and the writers referred to by the author. Both can be useful in helping you to find specific things you need (e.g. the work of a particular theorist that you want to refer to in your work).

○ Journal articles – most journal articles include an abstract at the beginning. The purpose of an abstract is to give the reader an outline of everything that is included. This helps the reader to decide whether or not they want to read the whole paper. When reading journal articles, always read the abstract first and then decide whether or not you want to read the whole thing, parts of it, or none of it.

○ Websites – we discussed the importance of only using reputable websites in Theme 4.2, but when you have found ones that you are confident about, remember that they are often organised under headings and that you can use the search facility to find what you need.

It is also good to remember to use ebooks; these fall into two categories. First, many widely used text books are available to students as ebooks through their online library. This means you can access them from anywhere and use the search facility to find what you need. This is often easier and quicker than looking at the book itself, especially when you need to scan it. The contents pages and index will be easy to use and you can print relevant pages if you feel you need to do so. However, some students prefer not to read everything on a screen and like the feel of an actual book. Remember too that when you leave university you will lose your IT access and, thereby, your access to ebooks.

Second, there are also ebooks available via internet search engines that allow you to look at the contents, references and a small selection of pages of a book. These can be helpful, as often they will give you an idea of how useful the book itself will be and whether or not you need to borrow it from the library or even buy a copy. They can also be beneficial if you are looking for a particular thing which happens to be on one of the selected pages. However, they also have downsides; for example, it can be very frustrating to be in the middle of reading something you really need only to find that the next page is not part of the selected sample. Recently published books tend to have a very small amount that is available – authors have to make a living after all!

In the early days of university, you might well feel that you need to read everything; for example, a whole book or article. This is definitely not the case! It is much more important to learn what you need to read and to read that. This isn't easy, especially in the early days, but will be a vital skill that will help you to achieve your academic goals.

Try this   Look at one of your recommended text books and identify a question or a task you have been set. Now decide which parts of it you need to read first. Use the contents page and the index to help you decide.

Making useful notes

Having decided what to read next and written down some goals or key questions to make sure that your reading is active, it will soon be time to take some notes. Note taking (whether by hand or on some kind of electronic device) is useful because it helps us to concentrate, and to clarify and consolidate our understanding (Bedford and Wilson, 2013). In addition, if we then have a clear record to go back to, we don't need to re-read the whole piece again, which is another time saver.

Here are some tips for note taking.

- Once you have read something (maybe a section or two of a chapter to start with), go back to the goals or key questions that you have set and use these as headings to write some notes.
- Make sure your notes are what they say they are – notes. They don't have to be in full sentences; you can use words and abbreviations that you understand and nobody except you needs to be able to make sense of them at this point.
- If you are struggling to make notes, go back and re-read the work to see if you can make more sense of what you have read. If so, you will then be able to make more notes and if not, it is probably a good idea to discuss this with your module tutor, especially if it seems to contain a key concept.

Notes should always be written in your own words because this is what helps your understanding. When things get difficult it can be very tempting to copy exactly what the author has written. There are two important reasons for not doing this: first, it will not help your understanding to develop, and second, unless you make a specific note (e.g. by highlighting what you have written) you might find yourself copying this into your written work, which would constitute plagiarism (see Theme 7.1).

There are times when you will want to quote directly from what an author has written to illustrate a particular point you are making in a piece of written work. This will often help to reinforce what you are saying and make your argument even stronger. So early on, start to look out for phrases and sentences that you might want to use as quotations in your work. This can be difficult at first but should get easier as you gain more experience. But here are some things that are good to avoid.

○ Direct quotations that are too long – good quotations are usually relatively short. It is impossible to say exactly how long a direct quotation should be, but a good 'rule of thumb' is that it should be no longer than two lines. If your quotation is longer than that it might be too long; in which case, you will probably need to paraphrase part of it and choose the specific words from it that are key to your argument.

○ Don't forget to note down the page number – you will need to include this when referencing. Forgetting to note it down and realising later means that you will need to go back and find it – this is an absolute pain! It also wastes precious time that you probably won't have at that point, as this often happens close to an assignment deadline.

Many students use coloured pens to highlight key points when reading. This is not a bad idea but here are some words of caution.

○ Highlighting does not help your understanding very much. It just helps you when you go back to re-read things.

○ It is not always easy to remember why you have highlighted something, so you may well need to make notes in the margins as well.

○ In a very useful chapter or paper you may well be tempted to highlight far too much. Later you will no longer be able to distinguish the most important points.

Most tutors will say that it is good to take notes. Whether you take them by hand or use an electronic device doesn't really matter, so long as you can find your notes and understand them. However, most of us can type more quickly than we can write by hand. This means that handwritten notes will probably take longer to make, but the process of doing it gives us more thinking time, which means that we might well understand and remember more of what we have read.

Try this   Choose a key chapter from one of your recommended textbooks. Now think about why you are reading it and write down some goals. Refer to a set question or task if you have one. You could also formulate some questions yourself in relation to where you hope to gain some new insights. Read the chapter and write some notes in your own words under your headings and questions.

Activity Look at one of the assignments you will have to write in the near future. Make some notes on relevant sources under the following headings.

○ Books
○ Chapters in edited collections
○ Academic journal articles
○ Websites

If appropriate you could also add archives, newspapers and magazines to your list. You may be able to think of other resources too that are appropriate to your academic discipline (e.g. exhibitions, performances).

Case study: Swamped by reading

Joel is coming to the end of his first term at university and is beginning to feel swamped by the amount of reading he needs to do. He is spending quite a bit of time on it but finds it very difficult to concentrate and is easily distracted. In addition, he is finding some of the reading difficult to understand. He decides to book an appointment with one of the academic support tutors based in the library.

Joel explains the situation to the tutor, who helps him to go through his module reading lists to identify some of the key readings he needs to focus on. He also encourages Joel to speak to each of his module tutors for their advice on key readings. The tutor also asks him about his strategies for effective reading and Joel soon realises that he is tending to focus on the most difficult texts. He was a strong student at school and feels that he should be able to do this. The tutor encourages him to take small steps and to choose some readings that he finds easier to help him to work towards the more difficult ones. Joel agrees to do this and soon begins to find the reading more enjoyable. As time goes on, he begins to feel more confident in his understanding of more difficult texts and makes sure to ask the module tutor for clarification if there are key concepts that he doesn't understand.

Top tip **Annotated bibliographies**

When reading a number of academic texts, compiling an annotated bibliography can be a very helpful thing to do as part of a strategy for taking effective notes. An annotated bibliography is a list of things you have read (e.g. books, chapters, journal articles) referenced in the appropriate style. Each reference is followed by a short description (usually about 150 words) of the text. Compiling an annotated bibliography will help you to:

○ Remember what you have read by keeping a record of it
○ Find things that you read earlier more easily or
○ Practice referencing in the appropriate style.

So, even if you haven't been asked to write one, why not have a go at doing it anyway; you might find it really helpful. Remember that you can take it along to a tutorial meeting or a seminar for reference.

Theme 5

Critical writing

This section will:

- ○ Help you to understand the term critical writing
- ○ Examine how you can develop a good argument
- ○ Enable you to use academic language more easily
- ○ Help you to evaluate different types of assessed written work
- ○ Consider how to proof read and check your work carefully before submission.

I write to discover what I know. – **Flannery O'Connor (1925–1964) American novelist, short story writer and essayist**

What is critical writing?

Theme 3 considered various aspects that are relevant to the topic of critical thinking, and at this point it is worth going back to re-visit these. As we move on to the area of academic writing, it is clear that assessed written work that gains high marks is usually analytical rather than descriptive. It should be well-argued and balanced and consider the evidence available.

So, what are the characteristics of critical writing? Here are some pointers that you can use as criteria to assess your own work, and you might be able to think of more from your own field of study.

○ Clear – your writing needs to be easy to understand. However, this does not mean that it should be simple or simplistic. If you can't understand what you have written, the person marking it probably won't be able to either!

○ Concise – try not to use 20 words when 10 will do. You will be surprised how quickly your word count runs out, especially if it's a large topic.

○ Coherent – there should be a flow to your writing which makes it easy for the reader to follow.

○ Balanced – it should not be one-sided but should give both sides a fair hearing.

○ Confident – again this means presenting your arguments clearly, and strongly too.

○ Supported by evidence – this usually means from published work, from your experience, or from research, depending on your academic discipline.

○ Clear conclusions – having 'weighed up' the arguments, this means being prepared to state your own considered views and not 'sitting on the fence' the whole time.

○ Not dogmatic or opinionated – this means recognising the limitations of your own work.

One key aspect of critical writing is the use of paragraphs; these act as tools that structure a whole piece of academic work. When used well, they break the work down into manageable parts for the reader and can aid the flow and coherence of the work. Here are some tips to help you in this area. Paragraphs should be:

○ Focused – think about the argument you are making. In each paragraph you should **Introduce** the point you wish to make, make the **Point** with the **Evidence** to support it, and **Reflect** on it critically (IPER).

○ Not too long – as a general rule, if a page contains only one paragraph, that paragraph is probably too long. Paragraphs are designed to help the reader to follow your arguments easily, and if a paragraph is too long, the reader will probably lose track of the point. If the point you are making is detailed and lengthy, think about how you can break it down into more than one paragraph to make it more digestible.

○ Not too short – there is a well-known phrase 'one sentence does not make a paragraph' and this is a good 'acid test' to apply to your work. In addition, you might be someone who presses the 'return' key too frequently (e.g. at the end of each sentence) and whilst you might not mean to start a new paragraph, it looks as if you do. The reader then becomes confused about whether you are starting a new paragraph or just a new sentence; all of this can make your work appear disjointed and spoil the flow of it.

Remember that critical writing is a skill and one that will develop over time as your studies progress. So, it is something that you will need to keep working at. Many universities employ staff who specialise in supporting students' academic development (e.g. learning consultants, writing consultants, academic support tutors) and it is well worth finding out about the support they can offer.

A strong piece of academic writing will usually have a central argument threaded throughout that will give the piece coherence. As you start the writing process, it is good to be clear about what this is, so that you will be able to keep the focus of the whole piece sharp. However, remember that the actual process of writing helps our understanding (see Theme 4.5), so don't expect to understand everything when you start to write, otherwise procrastination can easily take hold of you (see Theme 2.4).

Finding your central argument will always be important when starting to write your piece of work, even when planning it (see Theme 6). Your central argument describes your overall position on a particular subject. This is different from being argumentative, which implies that you are arguing for or against something almost for the sake of it. Your central argument is rather like a thread that runs right through your work, and it can emerge in several ways. Here are a few of them and you might be able to think of more from your own academic discipline.

○ From the assessment task or question itself
○ From your lectures, seminars and tutorials
○ From key texts you have read
○ From your experience (e.g. if you are on a professional course)
○ From discussions with other students.

Once you have found the central argument you wish to make, try writing it down in words that are easy to understand and remember to keep it short. One useful tip is to write it on a sticky note and then to keep it in a prominent place (e.g. on your computer screen). You will then be able to go back to it easily as you are writing, particularly when you find yourself losing track or going off at a tangent. One tried and tested way of writing your central argument is to phrase it as a statement that you will try and respond to in a balanced way throughout your piece of work.

The next step is to break the central argument down into its component parts and to think about the points for and against. Doing this may well help to give a preliminary structure to your writing. In Theme 3.5 we discussed the nature of analysis and the value of engaging in a debate in your work by presenting advantages alongside the disadvantages, rather than all the advantages followed by the disadvantages, and the same applies here. Below is an everyday example showing the arguments for and against eating an egg for breakfast, which should help you to see how to do this.

Central argument – everyone should eat an egg for breakfast

For	Against
Eggs are a good source of protein and low in fat	Eggs increase the level of cholesterol in your blood, which is linked with heart disease
Eggs are easy to cook	Not everyone likes cooking or has cooking facilities (e.g. people who have been evicted from their homes and are being housed in temporary accommodation)
Eggs are tasty	Some people don't like eggs
Eggs fill you up	Some people don't feel hungry when they wake up and can't eat a lot of breakfast
Eggs are quick to cook	Some people have to leave the house very early in the morning and have no time to cook
Eggs are full of vitamins	If someone is getting enough vitamins in their diet, their body will dispose of any extra vitamins they don't need

Remember that all the points above would need to be justified and supported with evidence (Metcalfe, 2006). In the example above, this evidence might well come from research reports and reliable websites, such as the National Health Service (NHS).

Try this　Choose a piece of work that you need to begin soon, or one that you are already working on, and think about your central argument. Phrase it as a statement and write it on a sticky note. Like the example above, now break it down into its component parts in the table below.

Central argument	
For	Against

Theme 5.3 Using academic language confidently

Academic language is very different from the language we use in everyday speech and using it can seem strange at first, especially if you are not used to it. However, it is good to remember that language is a powerful tool and using it well can enhance your argument and give an air of confidence to your work. Overall this should mean higher marks, which is always good news! The table below shows some dos and don'ts and it is well worth keeping a close eye on these.

Do	Don't
Use the third person as generally this creates a confident voice. So, 'it is useful to consider' sounds much stronger than 'I think that'.	Use the first person unless you are specifically asked to do so. Some written pieces might ask you to reflect on your experiences, so writing in the first person might be more appropriate. If in doubt, always check with the person who will be marking your work.
Write in full.	Use contractions. These are the ways we shorten things in spoken language (e.g. it's, that's, can't, won't) and should be avoided wherever possible.
Use words in full (e.g. television, quotation).	Abbreviate words (e.g. TV, quote).
Be careful with grammar and punctuation. Remember that your word processor can help you here so be sure to check all the prompts (e.g. wavy lines under words and phrases).	Overuse punctuation, in particular exclamation marks. These minimise the impact of your argument and suggest that you do not take it seriously; so why should anyone else?
Write in full sentences. As a minimum every sentence needs a subject and a verb.	Write incomplete sentences that do not have a verb.
Write in a tentative way. Remember that there are always at least two sides to an argument, so phrases like 'it is possible that', 'it could be argued that' and 'it appears that' will be useful.	Write in a dogmatic way. Avoid phrases like 'this is correct because', along with words like 'never', 'always' and 'obvious'.
Use language that is acceptable from the point of view of equality (e.g. fire fighter, police officer, humanity).	Use gender specific language (e.g. fireman, policeman, mankind).

Here are two further points.

- You also need to think about the tenses of the verbs you are using. If you are considering work published some time ago that still has an impact today, use the present tense. For example

  'Smith's work shows that ...' or 'The work of Jones illustrates ...'

  If you are examining a piece of published research, use the past tense. For example

  'Smith's study showed that ...' or 'The study that Jones carried out demonstrated ...'

- Avoid colloquialisms. These are words and phrases we use in everyday speech that are too informal for a piece of academic writing (e.g. 'it's okay because', 'it goes without saying', 'as clear as a bell').

Writing in a more formal academic style may appear strange, and even be difficult at first. As Burns and Sinfield (2012:257) argue, 'The essay ... is ... about learning to communicate in concise, targeted writing: if we can communicate our ideas effectively, we will get better marks'. So, all the effort should be worth it when it comes to the marks that you will get in the end.

Try this   Make a list of words that you might use when writing in an academic style; use the internet to research this if you feel you need to do so.

Different types of assessed written work

As part of your programme of study you are likely to be asked to complete different types of assessed written work. Setting a range of assessment tasks means that more students have the chance to excel. In addition, some assessment methods can prepare students well for things they might have to do in the workplace, or as part of the selection process for a job or internship. When working on these different assessed pieces of work, it is good to be aware of what makes each of them strong. Here is a list of the main types of assessment used and some pointers to help you to submit high quality work. You might be able to think of more from your own academic discipline.

○ Essays – these are perhaps the most well-known of all the assessment methods used. A strong essay will have a clear focus, present strong arguments and end with a robust conclusion. The language used throughout will be strong and confident. Most importantly, it will address the question or task that has been set; it is worth remembering that the main reason people fail a piece of work is because they fail to answer the question. This goes for other pieces of assessed work too.

○ Examinations – a whole theme is devoted to these (see Theme 9).

○ Projects – these are often larger pieces of work that involve some independent research. Many of the points made above in relation to essays will be important here too; often a project will have some practical elements and might be written up in the form of a report.

○ Dissertations or Independent Studies – many students complete these in their final year of undergraduate study. During this period, you work with a supervisor who helps you to make progress. Be sure not to leave everything to the last minute; it is easy to think that you have lots of time, but it can easily run out on you. Checking your work and proof reading will be important too (see Theme 5.5).

All university students spend lots of time working on their assessment pieces. Sometimes it is difficult to estimate how long a particular piece of work will take, especially if you have not been asked to do this kind of work before.

Most people underestimate the amount of time it will take them to complete a piece of work, so it is always good to allow yourself plenty of time. If it turns out to be too much and you finish early, you can always reward yourself with something like seeing friends or watching that film you have been hoping to see for some time.

Try this   Look through your assessment tasks for this term or
semester and make a list of them. Are there any in
particular that you feel might be difficult, or that are
unfamiliar to you? If so, who might you be able to discuss
them with?

Proof reading and editing

Shortly before you submit a piece of written work it will be important to proof read it, to edit it and to check it for any errors. Editing means reading your work thoroughly and making changes that you feel will improve it. Proof reading means examining what you have written very carefully to find and correct typographical errors and mistakes in grammar, style, and spelling. Here are some helpful tips.

- Editing – this is often done best throughout the process of writing a piece of work. After taking a break from your work, you will often re-read what you have written to get back into the flow of writing. This is often a useful opportunity to edit what you have written, and asking yourself some questions at this point can be helpful. For example, 'Have I kept to one main topic or argument per paragraph? Is my argument clear? Could I use fewer words to make my points more clearly?'

- Not too early – proof reading is one of the final tasks you will need to do; doing it too early can waste valuable time as you might correct work that later you decide to exclude through more editing.

- Not too late – leaving proof reading and editing until the last minute can mean that you do things in a rush, don't have enough time to make the changes you would like to make and miss errors that you would have spotted, given a bit more time.

- Set the text aside and go back to it later – if you have just finished writing your final draft, take some time out and go back to it later. If you start to proof read it straightaway, you may well not see the mistakes; it is very easy to see what you want to see rather than what is actually there. Even if you only have time for a half-hour break before proof reading, it will help.

- Read your work aloud – this will slow you down and means you are more likely to spot places where your work doesn't seem to make sense.

- Consider printing your work out rather than reading from a computer screen – this can help with issues of presentation and layout.

○ Consider asking someone else to proof read your work for you – this could be anyone with a good command of English. To protect yourself from plagiarism, it is best not to ask a fellow student on the same course as they could deliberately or unintentionally copy parts of your work.

○ Use all the tools provided by your word processor – be sure to check anything that has a wavy line underneath it and correct it if necessary. Don't forget to make sure that you use the relevant setting (e.g. English UK).

Taking a bit of time with all of the above is time well spent and remember, it could mean the all-important difference between degree classifications, or gaining a pass or a fail mark.

Activity   Examining a sample of weak academic writing

Here is a short extract from some weak academic work. Make some notes on why you think it is weak and how it could be improved. Be sure to mark all the errors on it too.

'Smith's report show many things that are wrong in our society. Vandalism, stealing and graffiti. This is all because people do not know the difference between right and wrong. Keeping a tidy environment is needed for people to be happy and healthy. I think this is very important. Teachers need to tell children how to behave. Parents needs to show their kids how to behave and discipline them when they go wrong. This means telling them off and making them sit on the naughty step. It is always wrong to hit children.'

Case study: Proof reading

Siobhan has an essay to write and has almost finished writing her first draft. She feels generally happy with what she has written and wants to start proof reading it for errors. But because she has spent so much time on it, she is worried that she might not see the mistakes she has made. The feedback on the work she submitted last semester stated clearly that it contained lots of errors, and she is keen to do better this time. She decides to discuss this with an academic support tutor at one of their clinic sessions.

At the clinic the tutor makes some suggestions regarding how Siobhan might get some help in this area. The tutor tells her about study support workshops available in the library and explains that Siobhan can take along a sample of her work and staff will look at it for her. The tutor also suggests asking a friend from another course to look at her work and offering to look at theirs too. This way they could both improve together. The tutor warns Siobhan strongly against asking someone on her own course to do this, in case they are tempted to copy her work even though they might not intend to do this. Siobhan decides to act on both of the suggestions to try and make some improvements in this important area.

Top tip   How to structure an assignment

All assignments need to have a clear structure as this makes them easier to read. Most university assessment criteria will include marks for structure, so a strong structure will help you to gain more marks. Most good assignments have a beginning, a middle and an end.

○ Beginning – make sure your work has a clear introduction. This is a vital signpost for the reader and helps them to know what to expect. A good introduction will highlight your central argument and outline the 'ground' that you will cover. Keep it fairly short and concise.

○ Middle – this is the main body of your piece of work, made up of paragraphs. Each paragraph should make a particular point and should not be too long (ideally no longer than half to three quarters of a page).

○ End – make sure you write a clear conclusion, otherwise your work will stop too abruptly and seem unfinished. A good conclusion will include a discussion of your overall position; it is not a time for 'sitting on the fence' as this will weaken the overall impact of your work.

The first and last sentences of any assignment are often the most difficult to write. Don't feel you have to write them first as they can be a 'stumbling block'; you can always add them later.

Theme 6

Getting ready for assessment

This section will:

○ Help you to understand assessment criteria

○ Help you to recognise the value of self-assessment

○ Enable you to appreciate different levels of study and grading systems

○ Help you to think about different assessment methods and understand what they demand

○ Examine what you need to do to get 'a good degree'.

Knowing is not enough: we must apply. Willing is not enough: we must do. – **Goethe (1749–1832) German writer and statesman**

Theme 6.1 Understanding assessment criteria

Tutors use assessment criteria when marking your work to help them reach a robust and considered judgement of the grade they are awarding. Assessment criteria also enable staff to mark your work consistently; this is particularly important if work is being marked by more than one tutor, which is often the case when there are large numbers of students taking a particular module. Assessment criteria are clear descriptions of the knowledge, understanding and skills that tutors look for when marking your work.

Understanding them is an important first step in getting ready for assessment. Unless you are familiar with the assessment criteria being used, you will not be clear about what tutors are looking for and will not know how to gain high marks. Many universities publish their criteria to make them known to everyone involved in the assessment process.

Here are some key points to help you to become familiar with assessment criteria.

○ Know where to find them – often they are included in important documents accessible online via the VLE. They might be contained in a document called a Programme Handbook or Course Handbook, and in module handbooks.

○ Know what they look like – assessment criteria can vary in the way they are presented, but many are laid out in grids (sometimes referred to as rubrics; see the example below) or lists that show the criteria themselves (e.g. focus on the task or answering the question, clarity of reasoning and style, referencing) and descriptions of what you need to do to gain marks within marking bands. At undergraduate level, the pass mark is usually 40% and the degree bands are often

40–49% Third class honours

50–59% Lower second class honours (2:2)

60–69% Upper second class honours (2:1)

70%+ First class honours (1st).

Criterion	100–80 Excellent	79–70 Very good	69–60 Good
Coherence and organisation of assignment	Strong logical organisation and coherence enhances fulfilment of the assignment objectives	Demonstrates logical organisation and coherence	Demonstrates sound, thoughtful organisation

59–50 Sound	40–40 Satisfactory	39–30 Fail	19–0 Fail
Demonstrates generally sound, conventional organisation	Shows limited organisation	Poorly presented and structured but partially understandable	Disorganised and/or incoherent

Each criterion will contain a description of what a piece of work looks like within each of the bands. So, it will describe the focus of a piece of work if a mark of 40–49%, 50–59% and so on is given. An example of assessment criteria at Level 4 from my own university (Canterbury Christ Church) under the heading of Presentation and Style is shown on the previous page.

○ Know how they are weighted – assessment criteria are not always weighted equally. In some pieces of work, certain criteria might carry more marks (e.g. in an essay, critical reasoning will be more important than in a practical piece of work).

Assessment criteria are provided for you to use and are a vital tool in helping you to produce work that is focused and appropriate. If you are finding it hard to locate them, or are having difficulty understanding them, be sure to ask one of your tutors, and make sure you become familiar with them.

Try this   Look on your VLE and find the assessment criteria being used to mark your work. If there is anything you don't understand, be sure to ask someone.

The value of self-assessment

In general, students understand the purpose of assessment that is carried out by tutors. In short, assessment is all about 'show you know' and provides you with an opportunity to demonstrate knowledge, skills and understanding. However, self-assessment is much less common and can be a useful tool for your learning and development. The table below highlights some key points about self-assessment; what it is and what it isn't.

Self-assessment is	Self-assessment is not
An opportunity to become more familiar with the assessment criteria used to mark your work	An opportunity to argue or disagree with your assessment criteria
A chance to reflect on the strengths and limitations of your work	A chance to defend your work
An opportunity to make a considered judgement about your work and to compare that with the mark given	An opportunity to mark your own work to get the grade you think you deserve
A chance to learn about how you could improve your work in the future	A chance to complain about a mark given
Helpful in understanding what tutors are looking for in assessed work	A means of asserting what tutors should be looking for in assessed work and why they should give you more marks

Self-assessment can be done in a number of different ways; it could be built into a module and be part of a course requirement or could be something that you do for yourself. Either way it can be a useful tool for your learning, as it puts you in the position of applying the criteria that will be used by tutors. This 'gets you into the shoes' of the assessor and helps you to see more of what they are looking for. You will then be able to evaluate more accurately what makes a good piece of work and where you might fall down.

Try this   Now try doing a piece of self-assessment. Look at a piece of work that you will be submitting soon; read it carefully and use your assessment criteria to make a judgement about its quality. Where are its strengths and how could it be improved? Make some notes here.

Levels of study

The majority of degree programmes involve three years of study (six years if you are a part-time student) and it is useful to understand that this means studying at different levels as you progress through your course. Before they start university, most people will have successfully completed studies at Level 3 (e.g. A Levels, International Baccalaureate, BTEC, Access course), although some will have taken a foundation year (Level 0). The levels of study involved to gain a degree are as follows.

○ Level 4 – Year 1 of a full-time course (Years 1 and 2 of a part-time course)
○ Level 5 – Year 2 of a full-time course (Years 3 and 4 of a part-time course)
○ Level 6 – Year 3 of a full-time course (Years 5 and 6 of a part-time course)

Many people say that they experienced a big 'jump' in their education from Level 2 (e.g. GCSE) to Level 3 in relation to the demands of the academic work required. Starting university means taking another leap forward and working at the next level up (Level 4). In addition, each year (or two years if you are a part-time student) of undergraduate study will mean moving up another level, and as a result you need to expect the work to become more demanding as you progress.

Universities publish their assessment criteria (see Theme 6.1) at each level, so be sure to familiarise yourself with all of the levels (4, 5 and 6) at the appropriate time.

Try this   Have a look at the assessment criteria for your course for Levels 4, 5 and 6. How do they differ? How do they become more demanding as you progress through the levels?

Different types of assessed work

In Theme 5.4 we looked at a range of different methods for assessing written work. However, not all assessed work is written, and depending on your academic discipline, you might be asked to do some of the following.

○ Presentations – many students are asked to present their work to their tutors and sometimes their peers as well. Some important tips are given on this in Theme 8.5.

○ Practicals – these are common in scientific programmes, and artistic and creative areas. Good time management will be particularly important here (see Theme 2) as many hours can be lost in the laboratory or art studio. Be sure to keep an eye for detail and to present work that is 'polished'.

○ Exhibitions – a final degree show is an important aspect of most art and design degrees and often carries a large number of marks towards the final degree classification. Thorough preparation will be vital, and be sure to find out how you will need to display your work at the show itself as this will be important.

○ Performances – these are key for creative arts students (e.g. music, dance, drama) and lots of practice will be required. You will also need to work on managing your stress levels (see Theme 9.5).

Sometimes practical aspects like the ones above can be combined with written work; for example, delivering a presentation or performance and writing a critical reflection on how you felt it went. This is another form of self-assessment. In such cases, be sure to find out about the weighting of the marks being given (how many for the presentation or performance and how many for the written piece) and divide your time appropriately. It is very easy to spend lots of time on practical aspects and neglect the written parts. This is a mistake if the division of marks is 50/50. For a written element, remember that tutors are looking for critical reflections on what went well and what could be improved or done differently. A critical reflection that states that you would do everything exactly the same again is unlikely to get you a high mark.

As a general rule, all assessments fall into the following two categories.

1 Formative – these pieces of work inform you and your tutors about your progress. The marks gained do not 'count' towards your degree or your marks for the year, but they offer a useful guide as to how well you are doing.

2 Summative – the marks for these pieces of work count towards your final total, either for the year or for your degree.

When completing any piece of assessed work be sure to find out if it will be formatively or summatively assessed. It is easy to fall into the trap of thinking that formative assessments are not important when they can give you a valuable opportunity to get some feedback on your work in order to improve it.

Try this   Take some time to look at any assessed work you have to do this semester that is not written. Think about your strengths and weaknesses and start to plan your time.

What you need to do to get 'a good degree'

In the activity at the end of Theme 1 you looked at what you were hoping to achieve by the end of your time at university, including the classification of degree you would like to be awarded. Now is a good time to look back at this and consider whether or not you might amend your goals.

Getting 'a good degree' is important, but how would you define this? For many students 'a good degree' means achieving either a first class honours or upper second and it is important to understand how you might achieve this. Here are some important principles to bear in mind.

○ On most degree courses Level 4 work is assessed and must be passed. However, the marks themselves don't 'count' towards your final degree classification for a number of reasons. Many students take time to settle at university, especially if they have moved away from home, and this relieves pressure in the early weeks. At this level many of the foundations are laid for strong academic study; for example, critical reading, research skills and robust writing. It is a good time to experiment with different approaches without the fear of low marks bringing down your marking average, and remember to check if the work you are being asked to do is formative or summative (see Theme 6.4).

○ At Level 5 things start to count and it is good to find out how much of your work at this level goes towards your final degree classification. On many courses this figure is 40% but it is always wise to check this for yourself as it can vary from course to course.

○ At Level 6 everything counts and overall your work at this level often adds up to about 60% of your total degree classification. In particular, make sure you are aware of modules that carry a larger number of credits than others. For example, typically a dissertation or independent study will carry more than a taught module, so you will want to allocate more time to it. For many students this particular aspect is 'the final push' in relation to course work.

○ Working out your final degree classification for yourself can be a tricky business, as it is usually not as simple as working out averages. Some universities have online calculators to help you to do this. Advice varies on whether it is good to use these or not; they can give you a clear idea of what you need to achieve but you can become disheartened if they do not give you the answer you are hoping for.

○ Many universities operate a system called 'compensation' where the lowest module mark at Levels 5 and 6 is set aside. This is to allow for the fact that any student can 'fall down' in one module and means that one low mark does not spoil their chances of getting 'a good degree'.

Whatever happens, achieving a degree will be one of your biggest achievements so far, so it is worth celebrating it. It will always involve hard work and is something that no one can ever take away from you.

Activity   Using feedback to gain higher marks

Look at the feedback you have received on your assessed work so far. In particular, look at the feedback that you got in relation to referencing. Are there any particular aspects that show you what you need to work on? If so, what are they and how will you address them? Make a plan now, including any study skills sessions you might want to attend.

Case study: Understanding different HE levels

Raja is in the second year of his degree course and has just received the marks for the modules he completed in the first semester. These marks have come as a bit of a shock to him as some of them are significantly lower than the marks he got in his first year. He is feeling angry and decides to go and talk to the Programme Director to see if anything can be done about it.

During his meeting with the Programme Director, Raja explains how frustrated and angry he feels and says that this is not the kind of mark he is used to getting. He says he thinks that there must have been a mistake and asks for his work to be re-marked. The Programme Director explains that the standard of work expected this year is higher and goes through the Level 5 criteria with him to show him how the criteria are more demanding. She advises him that it is not possible to produce work of a similar standard at Level 5 and to expect the same mark as he achieved at Level 4. Raja realises that he will have to develop his work further to get the marks he would like.

The Programme Director also says that Raja's work cannot be re-marked and explains how the assessment process works. A sample of all the pieces of work has been second marked to check that the tutor has applied the assessment criteria consistently and fairly. This will also be looked at by the External Examiner who will give feedback. She explains that at this point some marks might be changed, but that this is rare and should not be expected. She encourages Raja to continue to work hard and to develop his work, so he can then gain the marks he is used to at the higher level. She also advises him to expect to work at an even higher level in the next academic year.

Top tip **Understanding the assessment brief**

Lots of students fail all kinds of assessments because they don't answer the question or address the task. This is where understanding the assessment brief becomes very important. Tutors write assessment briefs to help you to understand what is required, so you need to read them carefully and follow any guidelines that are given. Not doing this will mean that you put yourself at much greater risk of failure.

An assessment brief will typically include:

○ An outline of the task – watch out for key words, such as essay, report, presentation, project, as this affects what you are expected to produce
○ A list of the learning outcomes being assessed
○ Some detail regarding how marks will be allocated
○ A description of which assessment criteria will be used
○ Referencing requirements
○ Submission dates and arrangements.

An assessment brief will not tell you what to write, but it should guide you in the right direction. If at any point you are not sure about what is expected of you, be sure to ask. Always go back to the learning outcomes too and use them as a measure of whether or not you have kept to the brief.

Referencing

This section will:

- Demonstrate the importance of using the appropriate referencing system to avoid plagiarism
- Help you to understand what makes a strong reference list
- Emphasise the importance of 'dotting the i's and crossing the t's'
- Introduce you to some referencing tools
- Enable you to keep a record of the references you have used to save you time later.

> Details make perfection, and perfection is not a detail. – **Leonardo da Vinci (1452–1519) Italian painter, sculptor, designer, architect, engineer and scientist**

Referencing systems

All academic work builds on the work of others and referencing systems are designed to give credit to authors for the work they have done. Referencing your work also means that the tutors marking your work can check the sources you are using as the basis for your arguments. Failing to acknowledge the work of an author means that you are passing their work off as if it is your own. This can be done in different ways and can be intentional or unintentional.

○ Intentional – for example, deliberately copying and pasting from websites or ebooks, or by copying directly from printed material

○ Unintentional – for example by not referencing appropriately, or by not referencing at all.

Either way it is copying and thereby a form of cheating. Plagiarism is copying someone else's work or borrowing their ideas and is a form of literary theft. Another aspect of plagiarism is called collusion. This is when two or more students study together to produce work that is either identical or very similar. Whether plagiarism is intentional or not, all universities take it very seriously by imposing some heavy penalties.

Referencing your work well is important in order to avoid plagiarism. There are many different referencing systems used by universities (from Harvard to Chicago) and it is vital to know which particular referencing system your university (or faculty, or even course) asks you to use. Some systems are designed for particular academic disciplines; for example, you might be asked to use the Oxford Standard for the Citation of Legal Authorities (OSCOLA) if you are studying Law. Using a specialised system like this when required usually makes the task of referencing easier. You always need to be sure to use the one specified and if you are in doubt about which system to use, be sure to check with your module tutor or Programme Director early on in your studies. Spending lots of time working on a reference list to then find you have used the wrong system is always very frustrating!

Referencing accurately is all about following a formula; to do this well, you will need an accurate and reliable guide to help you, and an eye for detail. There are many good referencing guides available, so early on in your studies it will be good to identify one that suits you and that you find easy to use. Some students like to use an online guide, and, in this case, one good starting point is to look on your own university's website. If you don't find what you need there, don't be afraid to look at other university websites. Other students prefer to have a printed guide that they can keep and refer to as and when they need it. Printing an online guide is, of course, one option, or you could choose to invest a small amount in a publication like *Cite Them Right* (Pears and Shields, 2016). Remember to check your library catalogue as this could be available as an ebook. It is always good to remember that referencing guides can vary in their quality and there are poor guides available as well as good ones. If you are unsure about the quality of a particular referencing guide, do check with academic staff.

Try this Search online for a referencing guide that you find easy to use. Now look at your university's plagiarism policy; you should be able to access this online via your student portal or VLE.

What makes a strong reference list?

Many students ask how many references should be in a good reference list. This is a difficult question to answer as it depends on your academic discipline and the length of the piece of work that you are writing. However, as a general guide, a good reference list will usually reach double figures. It is not just the number of references that counts though, but the quality and range of them too. Here are some pointers to help you.

A strong reference list is:

○ Well balanced – it contains a range of books, chapters from edited books, academic journal articles and pieces from reputable websites (e.g. from professional bodies)
○ Current – it includes recent publications (e.g. published within the last five years)
○ Seminal – it includes publications that are still relevant even though they have been published for a good number of years.

A weak reference list is:

○ 'Flaky' – if it only contains websites
○ Dated – if it only contains publications over 10 years old
○ Incomplete – if it misses relevant seminal literature.

Putting a strong reference list together takes time as it requires some careful attention to detail (see Theme 7.3). It is a good idea to formulate your list as you go along, rather than leaving it until the end. As a deadline looms, you might need to work more quickly, and working on a detailed reference list is not something that is easy to do in a rush. In addition, you might forget where you found certain things and lose valuable time looking for them again.

It is also important to understand the difference between a reference list and a bibliography. A reference list is a list of all the publications you have referred to in your work. A bibliography is usually broader, and also includes things that you have read but not referred to. If you are unsure about whether you need to produce a reference list or a bibliography, be sure to ask a tutor.

Try this

Now find a reference list from a piece of work that you have submitted recently. Using the points made in Theme 7.2, how strong do you think it is? How could you strengthen it further?

Dotting the i's and crossing the t's

Putting together a good reference list means following a formula and having an eye for detail. There is no simple way of doing this or any totally reliable short cut; it's a question of careful precision. But why does this matter? One key reason is given in Theme 7.1, which is giving authors credit for their work. Another is making sure that you gain the highest marks you can for your assessed work. Most university assessment criteria include something about the quality and accuracy of your reference list. Gaining a high mark here can mean the difference between a grade boundary, and ultimately even a degree classification; so it is well worth the effort as it will count, and might make all the difference.

When you have found a good referencing guide to help you, it is then a case of following the formula carefully. Be sure to look out for the detail, for example

○ When to use capital letters
○ When to use italics
○ When to include page numbers
○ Making sure you use punctuation correctly (e.g. commas, full stops, colons).

Putting together a strong reference list is one important aspect of referencing and the other is referencing publications in the body of your work. Most referencing guides give advice on this too, and here are some more pointers.

○ If you are using the work of a particular author, you need to refer to them, even if you are not quoting from their work directly. Their surname and the year of the publication is usually sufficient (so no initials).
○ If you are quoting directly from someone's work, you should always include a page number, so the reader can refer back to it if they need to do so.
○ If something has been written by three or more authors, you need to use the 'et al.' convention. Some argue that the first time you refer to the work, you need to include all the surnames, and then 'et al.' in subsequent references, others use the 'et al.' convention throughout.

○ If an author is referring to the work of another author, you will need to use the 'cited in' convention. So, if Smith (2018) is writing about Jones (2008) in their work and you wish to refer to Jones, your reference will need to be Jones (2008, cited in Smith, 2018).

One aspect of a referencing system is where you will be asked to include references. Here are some common ones.

○ Within the text itself
○ In footnotes – these are at the bottom of the particular page (i.e. in the footer)
○ In endnotes – these are at the end of the whole document.

Again, if in doubt, do ask a member of academic staff.

Many people find referencing a chore, but one that is ultimately worthwhile for the reasons we have discussed. Overall, it's best not to rely on your memory, but always to use a reliable guide or tool.

There are many referencing tools available if you search online, and, as the term suggests, they can be very helpful when it comes to the task of referencing your work. Using a good tool can help you to save lots of time, as it will do most of the work for you. However, like referencing guides, some tools are much better than others. Some of the most common include RefWorks, EndNote, Zotero and Mendeley. Microsoft Word also has a built-in referencing tool under the Referencing tab and this can help you to make citations in the body of your work and to devise a reference list or bibliography.

Choosing a referencing tool that you will find easy to use is an important first step. As a first 'port of call' it is always best to use those that are recommended by your own university. Some universities have even devised versions of their own, and in such cases, it is usually best to use the one provided. Other universities recommend a number of different tools and in this case, you might need to try them to see which you find easiest. Remember, there are many free tools available online, but they are not all of good quality. Some will not find even key texts when you search on their system and others will give you incomplete details. For example, there are Harvard tools that give just the publisher (e.g. Sage) when actually the Harvard style asks for Place: Publisher (e.g. London: Sage). This means you will then need to look for the place yourself, which can be time consuming; without this your reference will be incomplete, and this will have a negative impact on your mark. Overall it can be as quick to put the whole reference together yourself using a guide.

Using a referencing tool can be time consuming initially, as it can take a while to get used to what you need to do. However, once you are familiar with it, most systems enable you to save all your references so you can access them later. This can save you lots of time further down the line, particularly if you know you will use certain references more than once during your programme of study. So, time spent learning how to use a tool and using it early on in your studies can be time well invested. In addition, a reliable tool will usually be much more accurate than a human being, as any of us can make mistakes when putting a reference list together.

Try this   Have a look at some online referencing tools and make a list of them here. Now think about the pros and cons of each and consider which you might try using. Which does your own university recommend? Which others look useful too?

Record keeping

Keeping a record of things you have read is useful, as you never know when you might need to refer to something in the future. There is nothing more frustrating than remembering that you have read something, but not knowing where to find it when you need it for an assignment. This will undoubtedly take up valuable time that you might not have at that particular point. Here are some tips to help you; they might save you some valuable time just when you need it.

○ If you decide not to use a referencing tool for storing your references, something as simple as a Word document with all your reference lists combined into one alphabetical list will be helpful. It's then a simple 'copy and paste' task as you build your new list.

○ Keep things quick and simple by scanning to your university email. Most universities have MFDs (multifunctional devices) and scanning is usually free. For example, scanning a few key pages from a book or article if you think you might need them for a direct quotation later on can be very effective. Scanning a book cover and the copyright page near the front that gives all the publication details could also be very helpful. Taking pictures with your smartphone can be just as effective.

It is also good to use your university IT account to its full potential. It will include your own personal storage space on a 'cloud', accessible from any internet linked PC. Be sure to keep your work in at least two different places just in case, and emailing it to yourself is another good 'backup'. Most universities offer IT training and if you feel your IT skills could be better, why not take the opportunity to go to a workshop? There are many online tutorials on offer too.

Activity   An example of poor referencing

Here is an example of poor referencing in the Harvard style. Using the details given in Theme 7.3 and a reliable referencing guide, find the mistakes and correct them. Even if you need to use a different system, this is a good exercise for developing an eye for detail. The answers to this are provided in the back of the book on page 176.

Adams, J., Hayes, J. and Hopson, B. (1976) *Transition: understanding and Managing personal Change*, Martin Robertson.

D. Bedford and E. Wilson 2013 *Study Skills for Foundation Degrees*, 2nd edn. Abingdon: Routledge.

Burns, T. and Sinfield, S. (2012) *Essential Study Skills: The Complete Guide to Success at University*, 3rd edn. London: Sage.

Clark, A. (2005) *IT Skills for Successful Study*, Basingstoke.

Cottrell, S. (2013) *The Study Skills Handbook*, London: Red Globe Press.

Covie, S. (2004) *The Seven Habits of Highly Effective People: Restoring the Character Ethic*, New York: Free Press.

Eales, L-J., Judge, B., MacCreery, E. and Jones, P. (2013) *Critical Thinking Skills for Education Students*, 2nd edn. London: Sage.

Honey, P. and Mumford, A. 2000 *The Learning Styles Helper's Guide*, Maidenhead: Peter Honey Publications.

Kleinbeck, U.,Quast, H-H and Hacker, H. *Work Motivation*, Brighton: Lawrence Erlbaum Associates.

Metcalfe, M. (2006) Reading Critically at University, London: Sage.

Pears, R. and Shields, G. (2016) *Cite Them Right*, 10th edn. Red Globe Press.

Smale, B and Fowlie, J. (2009) How to Succeed at University: An Essential Guide to Academic Skills and Personal Development, London: Sage.

Tomlinson, M (2017) 'Student perceptions of themselves as consumers of higher education' in *British Journal of Sociology of Education*, 38:4.

Case study: Being at risk of plagiarism

Sophie and Laura have known each other for a few years as they were best friends at school and college; they are now studying at university together. They have always found it helpful to study together as it really helps their motivation. They are used to sharing their ideas with one another, they work on assignments together and often proof read one another's work. For the past few months, Sophie has been struggling with some personal issues and Laura has been doing all she can to support her.

It is getting close to the next assignment deadline and Sophie is worried that she might not be able to complete the work in time. Laura shows Sophie the final version of her work, as she feels this is a good way of helping a close friend. She also offers to email the work to her, and Sophie is very grateful for the help. Having access to Laura's work means that Sophie is clearer about what she needs to do, so she meets the deadline successfully.

A week later, Sophie and Laura both receive letters asking them to attend a meeting with the Programme Director to discuss allegations of plagiarism. During the meeting the Programme Director explains that Turnitin has drawn her attention to high levels of similarity between the two pieces of work and asks them to explain how this might have come about. Laura explains what happened and emphasises that she was only trying to support Sophie who was having a difficult time. Sophie becomes tearful and says that she did not intend to copy Laura's work. She also explains that this is what they did regularly when they were at college together and that they were told this was okay. However, the Programme Director explains that the university has strict rules about plagiarism, which includes collaborating with another student. Their work is too similar and as a result they have both been awarded a fail grade; they are both asked to re-submit the work and, as it is a re-submission, their marks will be capped at 40%. Sophie disputes this as she feels it is unfair on Laura, but the Programme Director explains that using Turnitin means that every student signs a declaration that the work is their own. In this case it is not possible to say with absolute certainty which student wrote the work, so both have to be penalised. The Programme Director warns Laura about the dangers in sharing her work with another student.

Weaving references into your work

Supporting your arguments by referring to the published work of others is a skill that you will develop during your studies. Doing this well will help you to gain high marks against assessment criteria that relate to literature as well as the referencing criterion itself. In many instances, you will need to discuss the work of authors critically, focusing on the relative strengths and weaknesses. It is good to keep direct quotations short (no more than one to two lines) and not to rely on them too heavily.

As you prepare your assessed work, it is good to be clear about the references you want to include, and you could try the following approach. Start with a list of the names of all the authors you want to refer to. Using your reading lists, be sure to include all of those whose literature is essential; failing to include some of these could affect your marks negatively. Then move on to include others and those you have come across through your own wider reading; you can also draw on other research you might have carried out. Keep your list for your future records.

When you have completed the first draft of your work, go back to your list and tick off all of the authors and sources you have referred to. Look at what is left on your list; now go back to your work and be sure to refer to any essential texts that you have missed. You can then make decisions about the other remaining sources in relation to their importance.

Studying with others

This section will:

- ○ Demonstrate the value of study groups
- ○ Introduce you to the concept of peer mentoring
- ○ Discuss the value of team work
- ○ Discuss the pros and cons of group assessment
- ○ Examine the skills in delivering effective presentations.

> Alone we can do so little, together we can do so much. – **Helen Keller (1880–1968) American author, political activist, lecturer and the first deaf-blind person to gain a Bachelor of Arts degree**

The value of study groups

All programmes of study can be challenging at times and being part of a study group can be very helpful in a number of ways; here are some of them.

Being part of a group means:

○ you have support available from fellow students when things get tough. They can be particularly helpful as examinations approach (see Theme 9) and stress levels rise

○ you can compare notes from lectures and seminars

○ you can share your understanding of key concepts

○ you can share resources (e.g. books, articles)

○ you can learn from other people in the group as each member will have different strengths and weaknesses

○ you have good opportunities for discussion in a non-threatening environment.

The size and makeup of study groups is important for them to be effective. Most people agree that a good size is four to six people and it is important that everyone is studying on the same or similar course. However, triads (or groups of three) can work very well too. There needs to be a high level of trust between group members and a good level of commitment to the group. People need to get on well and enjoy spending time together; everyone learns more when they are having some fun!

Study groups can be more or less formal depending on what works best for those in the group. People living on or near the university campus can afford to be flexible in their approach, for example, spending an hour together, going off to study separately and then getting back together again later to discuss what they have achieved can work well. Those living at some distance will welcome more regular meetings at particular times of the day when everyone can attend. In all cases it will be important to be clear with one another about what the goals are so that meetings are purposeful. An effective group meeting usually lasts no longer than two hours; shorter than that and things might feel rushed, longer than that and you can lose focus and be distracted by other things. Finding a good place to meet will be important too and many university libraries contain rooms you can book in advance for study group meetings. Others have open areas where groups can meet more informally.

It is always important to be a good member of a study group. Nobody wants to be in a group which

- is dominated by one person who talks all the time
- involves someone who doesn't 'pull their weight'
- includes someone who regularly doesn't turn up and doesn't let anyone know that they aren't coming
- includes someone who 'takes' but doesn't 'give'.

Being part of a study group means that you will probably make some close friends who you can call on when you need it. For example, if you are ill and have to miss some lectures, someone in your group will probably be happy to share their notes with you. These may well be some of the people you celebrate with on graduation day!

Try this

Now think about who you might work well with in a study group and why. Are there people you might not work so well with? What could you do to ensure a positive working relationship with them?

Peer mentoring

Many universities offer peer mentoring schemes and it is well worth participating in one of these if you get the chance to do so, as they can be extremely valuable. Having a peer mentor as a first year student usually involves being paired with a student on a similar programme in their second or third year. This is someone who you can meet with to talk about things very informally and is often described as 'support for students by students'.

Having a peer mentor can be helpful for the following reasons:

- They have probably had similar experiences to you but are a few steps ahead.
- You can chat with them informally and ask basic things that you might not feel able to ask a member of university staff, such as where to find things on campus or how to find things on the VLE or in the library.
- On the academic side they can give you lots of useful tips on things related to managing your studies.
- They can also help if there are things that you don't understand in introductory modules, but that you feel embarrassed to speak to a lecturer about.
- They can offer support and encouragement when things get difficult e.g. when your results are not as good as you hoped.
- They know where to go to get more help when you need it and can point you in the right direction.
- It need not take a lot of time and can make all the difference to your motivation.

Many students value having a peer mentor, and once you have completed your first year successfully it might be that you want to sign up to be a peer mentor for a new student the following year. Some universities run eMentoring schemes which link students together before their course starts. This can be particularly valuable for students who are nervous about starting something new. Training will be offered, and being a peer mentor can be very satisfying, as well as being a great thing to be able to add to your CV.

Try this   Find out about your university's peer mentoring scheme and consider asking for a mentor. How could this particularly help you?

The value of team work

Many people recognise that an effective team will always achieve more than individuals working separately. This is because no individual is good at everything and working in a team means that you can play to everyone's strengths. Within a team one person's strength may well be another's weakness, so you should be able to make the most of everyone's strengths in order to achieve more.

On your course you might sometimes be asked to work in a team. This is different from working in a study group (see Theme 8.1) where you usually choose who you would like to work with. Often you are placed in teams and are asked to work together with people you might not ordinarily choose to work with; this can make team work more challenging. Many of the principles outlined on pages 117–18 also apply to working in a team, but here are some additional points to consider.

○ Unlike a study group, a team will usually need a leader to coordinate the work. This role is vital to the team's success and in the early phase you should discuss who might be best suited to taking this on.

○ People fulfil different functions in teams. Just like a football team, a team full of defenders will not score many goals or win many matches. Being clear about people's strengths and weaknesses and 'playing to these' will be important.

○ Teams are usually put together to carry out a project or to achieve some goals. It is good to be clear about these early on and to discuss how these can be achieved. This includes practical things such as when team meetings will take place and which aspects of the work will be done and when.

○ As the work progresses it will be useful to assign tasks to members of the team and to have a written record of what has been agreed with deadlines. That way it is easier to keep track of the whole exercise, and it means that people will be clearer about what they are expected to do.

Being a good team member is vital to the success of the team. Nobody wants to work with someone who is not committed, so be sure to play your part and encourage others to do so too.

Group assessment

Some modules include group assessment, and these can offer a good opportunity to work collaboratively with your fellow students. Like team work, a group in this instance will often be put together by the module tutor, so you may well not have a choice about who you work with. Group assessment is either formative or summative (see Theme 6.4) and typically you might be asked to work on some kind of project or task, and then to present the outcomes. This presentation could be oral (see Theme 8.5) or written.

Many students express frustration about the process of being assessed as a group; the main complaint is from students who feel they do all the work while others 'coast' along without much effort. This is particularly irritating when the group as a whole is awarded a mark rather than the individuals within it. If you are asked to undertake a task for a group assessment, it is good to bear the following things in mind.

○ Be sure to find out if a group mark will be awarded or whether different marks will be given to individual group members.

○ Be sure to find out if it is the task that is being assessed or the process of how the group has worked together. Sometimes it can be a combination of the two.

○ It really is important that everyone in the group 'pulls their weight' and an important part of bringing this about is to make sure that the work is divided equally between group members.

○ A supportive environment usually brings out the best in people and working together in the same place (e.g. the library) means everyone in the group will know how the work is progressing. If you can't all work in the same place, be sure to 'catch up' with one another whenever you can (e.g. after lectures).

○ Be ready to offer help if you can see that a group member is struggling, but don't 'let them off the hook'. Make sure they play their part by asking them to do something else.

○ If the group assessment involves a presentation (see Theme 8.5) make sure that this is shared. Asking one member of the group to do the whole presentation (even if they say they want to do this) puts a lot of pressure onto that person. In an assessed situation anyone can get more nervous than they anticipate. It is also then too easy to blame that person if the group doesn't get a good mark.

Group assessments are often one part of the assessment for a module. Sometimes you will also be asked to write an individual reflective evaluation of how your group worked together. Here, it is important to remember the difference between offering a critique and engaging in negative criticism (see Theme 3.4). Critique will evaluate the strengths and weaknesses of how the group worked together, and how they could have done things better. Negative criticism or boasting about having done all the work will not gain you many marks for your reflective evaluation.

Delivering an effective presentation

At times you might be asked to do an oral presentation of your work as part of the assessment process. This can be a nerve wracking experience, especially if it is part of your summative work, so it is good to bear the following 4 Ps in mind.

○ Preparation – thorough preparation is absolutely vital and it is always a mistake to think that you can go into a situation like this and 'play it by ear'. Even experienced presenters have 'come unstuck' by doing this, as their nerves take over on the day.

○ PowerPoint – if you put together a PowerPoint presentation, be sure to find out what is expected; whether you should include references or not. Be sure to make it visually attractive and professional and don't put too much text on each slide. Use bullet points instead of full sentences and remember that the person watching needs to be able to read it. They really don't want to sit and listen to you reading directly from it, so be sure to have some notes with you. Prompt cards can work very well and using them means it is easier to maintain some eye contact.

○ Practice – you will need to practice a presentation several times, especially because it will usually be timed. Be sure not to speak for longer than you are asked to; this is rather like exceeding a word count in a piece of written work and doing this will mean that you won't gain as many marks as you should.

○ Poised – this is about how you put yourself across. Thorough preparation will mean that you should know your material well, and this means you can be confident. Remember that presenting can be rather like acting, so you will need to speak more slowly than usual and make some eye contact with the person or people you are speaking to. But don't fall into the trap of thinking it is an audition for drama school! How you stand is important too in putting your work across confidently, so remember to keep your body language open (don't cross your arms or legs) and don't obstruct people's view of the screen.

Most people are nervous about delivering a presentation (Clarke, 2005) and, on one level, we all should be. When we are nervous, it's a sign that our adrenalin is 'kicking in' and this helps us to perform well. However, if we are too nervous, our nerves can get in the way and can stop us from delivering a good presentation. Here are some tips that can help you to feel calmer and remain in control of your nerves.

- Back to preparation – there really is no substitute for it.
- Have a backup – save your presentation in more than one place and email your presentation to yourself so you can access it easily and quickly; not being able to find it or access it is a recipe for disaster.
- Stay well hydrated – take a bottle of water with you; your mouth can get very dry when you are anxious.
- Be early – being late isn't worth thinking about as you will probably panic.
- Breathe – take some deep breaths.
- Get a good night's sleep – you probably won't present well if you are tired.

If you are asked to submit an evaluation of your presentation, be sure to make some notes immediately following it as this will help a lot. At this point it will be tempting to heave a huge sigh of relief, but spending just a few minutes to note down a few points will help in the long run because it will still be fresh in your mind.

Try this   Think about a presentation you have delivered recently. What were its strengths and how could you improve in the future? If you haven't ever delivered a presentation, think about one that you have seen. What was good about it and how would you improve it?

Activity   Building a good study group

Think about how you could try and form a study group to help you to keep your levels of motivation high and to make progress in your work. Consider such issues as who might be in it and why, when and where you might meet and how you could support one another in different ways. Why not try talking to a few people now?

Case study: A good study group

Jack, Claire and Leroy are all studying for a degree in Economics and have often spoken to one another after lectures and seminars. They all like to work in the library and often find that they bump into one another there. They begin to exchange ideas and one day Leroy suggests that they go for lunch together. Over the next few months they become good friends and often discuss their work to encourage one another. Before long they realise that they all benefit from the discussions they have, although they have never thought of themselves as a study group.

As their course progresses they meet more regularly, particularly as they work towards their assignment deadlines. Claire enjoys the mathematical aspects of the course and often spends time explaining these; as well as helping Jack and Leroy, this also helps her to understand these in more depth. Leroy is a strong academic writer and will often proof read Jack and Claire's work to help them to strengthen their academic language. Jack has a real eye for detail and will usually check everyone's references. They are always careful never to take someone else's work or ideas.

In their third year they all spend a lot of time working independently on their dissertations. This involves more time in the library and it is always good to see one another there. This helps their motivation a lot and they regularly meet up to discuss things as well as to have coffee and to go out and relax together. As their time at university comes to an end they plan what they will do on their graduation day. Claire suggests that they could all go out together after the ceremony with their families, and they all feel this is a good idea. On the day they enjoy celebrating together and are thankful for the support they have had and the great friendships they have made.

Top tip   **Common communication problems in groups**

Working in a group can be a very enjoyable experience when everyone works hard and gets on well. However, this doesn't always happen, and groups can easily become dysfunctional. One of the most common problems in groups is poor communication; for a group to work well there needs to be good communication between all the group members.

Communication is something that we all need to work at to make it effective and it is easy for individual group members to feel isolated and excluded. Some key points to remember are as follows.

- Use a quick and easy method to communicate with each other (e.g. via social media or email).
- Make sure that everyone is included in all messages.
- Keep messages short and to the point.
- Never complain about one group member to another in messages.
- Be supportive if you sense that some group members are struggling.

Making time for the group will be important. Don't forget that something as simple as having a coffee or lunch together can help you to bond as a group.

Theme 9

Examinations

This section will:

○ Discuss how to make a good revision plan

○ Help you to write good revision notes

○ Enable you to plan for an open examination

○ Discuss various aspects of practical examinations

○ Help you to manage your stress levels.

Our greatest weakness lies in giving up. The most certain way to succeed is always to try just one more time. – **Thomas A. Edison (1847–1931) American inventor and businessman, credited with developing devices such as the electric light bulb and motion picture cameras**

Devising a workable revision plan

When you know that exam time is coming into view, it is probably time to make a revision plan. Keeping in mind the old phrase 'to fail to plan is to plan to fail' is useful again at this point, and having a good plan in place helps in many ways, including the following:

○ It helps us to feel more in control – without a plan we can easily feel overwhelmed. Preparing for multiple exams is a big task and can often feel daunting; a plan makes things more manageable and do-able.

○ It gets things out of our heads – making some kind of visual plan means we can see what we have to do in front of us. It no longer whirls round in our head, getting bigger each day we think about it.

○ It helps to reduce stress – all exams are stressful as inevitably a lot rests on them. Having a good plan means that you are clearer about what you need to do and when you will do it.

So, what makes a workable revision plan and how do you devise one? Here are some key steps to follow:

1　As soon as your exam timetable is published, take a copy of it.

2　Look at the big picture first, so identify which exams take place when. This will give you pointers about what you need to revise and by when.

3　Then think about where you need to concentrate your efforts. Identify your weaker areas as you will probably need to give more time to these. But don't fall into the trap of neglecting your strengths as this is where you might well gain your highest marks.

4　Be sure to schedule any revision sessions with academic staff and go along. This means you can ask them to go through things that you are finding difficult to understand.

5　Then plan the days themselves and be realistic and flexible with what you think you can achieve. Most people work best in relatively short sessions, so keep an eye on how you work well. If you have a whole day for revision, be sure to break it down into slots of say one to two hours (or shorter depending on how you work best) and allow yourself breaks and some relaxation time. Don't plan to do too much, because if you then don't achieve it, you will feel demotivated. Remember too that very few people work well when they are tired.

6 The next important step is to try and keep to the plan. If you find that things are taking more or less time than you anticipated, be flexible and adjust your plan accordingly.

7 Don't forget to use your study group and your friends to encourage you. They will need your encouragement too, as exam times can be tough.

There is no such thing as a perfect revision plan. It doesn't matter if your plan is on paper in a notebook, on a chart on your wall, on a spreadsheet on your laptop or in a calendar on your phone. Do what suits you best but be sure not to lose it! Leaving your notebook containing your detailed revision plan on the bus can be devastating, so having a copy somewhere (even if it's a photocopy or scanned copy of a few pages of your plan) can be a life saver. Printing something off to have a physical reminder can also be very helpful as it's then more difficult to forget about it, get distracted and lose your focus. Ticking things off your plan or crossing them off once they are done is a great way of keeping yourself motivated. Also, be sure to mark the end date of your exams clearly so you can see your ultimate goal and plan how you will celebrate!

Try this   Look at your exam timetable and start to devise a workable revision plan.

Writing good revision notes

Most students agree that preparing good notes is an important part of the process of effective revision. We already know that writing helps us to understand things better (see Introduction, page ix) and in addition, research shows that we are much more likely to remember something if we write it down than if we simply read it. So, how do you write good revision notes? Here are some pointers.

○ Writing good revision notes actually starts with your lecture notes (see Theme 4.5). If you have good lecture notes, you will probably need to condense these in some way to formulate useful revision notes. Review your lecture notes to identify key topics and concepts and then summarise them. At this point it might be as simple as making a list of them. You might also have made notes as part of your assignment preparation, so don't forget to use these too.

○ Then start going through each key area to condense your notes into a shorter form. Don't forget to use readings and text books to make sure that you have covered the necessary ground.

○ You might then find that your notes are still relatively long, so don't worry if you need to repeat this process a few times. At each stage you will probably find that you remember more as you condense your notes further.

○ Summarise your notes; this could be by writing them onto cue cards that are easy and quick to read, by drawing mind maps or diagrams, or by putting key concepts and theories into tables with short explanations. Again, do whatever you find works best for you.

○ Make everything visual by using different colours. This can be different colour cards or paper, highlighting text or using different coloured pens. In the exam room it can be helpful to visualise where things are in your notes to aid your memory.

Many people find revision boring and it's easy to see why, as going over what you have learned already can be tedious. So why not draw on your study group? Having to explain something to someone else can be a very helpful way of being sure that you have understood it yourself. It might also support someone else if it is something they are finding difficult.

Try this   Now think about how you will make good revision notes.

Planning for an open exam

In many cases exams can seem like a test of what you remember, or of how fortunate (or unfortunate) you are in revising for the questions that appear on the paper. An open exam (sometimes called an open book exam) will often be a greater test of what you have understood and how you can apply your knowledge.

So first, what is an open exam? An open exam is one where you can usually take some notes into the exam room with you. Sometimes you might be permitted to take books with you too, hence they are often referred to as open book exams. You might be given the exam question (or questions) beforehand, or you might not, and either way preparation will be key to your success. Like unseen exams, they are timed.

Many people have little experience of doing an open exam, and how you prepare for one is quite different from revising for an unseen paper. Here are some of the important steps involved.

○ Check the relevant requirements – make sure that you have the exam question or questions if they have been issued and that you are clear about exactly what you will be allowed to take into the exam room. This might be a notebook or separate sheets of paper, and reference books.

○ Preparation – this is absolutely fundamental; don't underestimate the length of time this will take. The better your preparation, the more likely you are to gain a mark you will be pleased with.

○ Be concise – it is very easy to take too much information into an open exam and then to lose lots of precious time trying to find what you need. Your notes need to be short and very well organised; for example, you can use headings, bullet points and different colours to make things stand out. Consider using some kind of graphic organiser; this is a tool that can help you to organise your ideas and see the relationships between different theories and concepts. Because they are visual, they can really help you to recall what you need when you are in the exam room. You can find lots of examples of these online, so find some that suit you and try them out.

○ Beware of books – there may be certain types of exams (e.g. legal exams) where you will need to take certain books with you into the exam room. But in other instances, books can be a hindrance as they can become distracting. Often it works better to have effective notes with you that summarise key points from texts rather than having the books themselves.

○ Time yourself beforehand – do some practice questions using your notes, as doing this should show you roughly how long it will take you in the exam room.

Don't be fooled into thinking that open exams are an easy option; they are different and often just as demanding. With good preparation they should be less stressful, and in many cases staff will offer preparation sessions for open exams. Like all revision sessions, they are probably not worth missing, so be sure to get them into your calendar.

Preparing for practical exams

A wide range of degree courses include practical components and in these situations, you will be required to take some practical exams. You might be asked to do a practical exam individually, in a pair, or even in a group. Like all exams, you will need to prepare well for it and here are some key pointers to help you.

○ Be sure to arrive at the venue in good time, especially if it is unfamiliar to you.

○ Think carefully about what you will need to take with you. Pack your bag ahead of time and check with some of your fellow students to make sure you have absolutely everything you need.

○ When you get into the exam room, read through all the instructions very carefully. Remember to turn the page over in case there are more instructions on a second page.

○ Plan your answers and tasks carefully before you start working on them, so you can allocate your time appropriately.

○ Most importantly, focus on what you are doing. It's very easy to be distracted by others and to lose valuable time as a result.

Practical exams are all about assessing your skills as well as your knowledge and its application. Remember to practice before the exam so you will be able to complete tasks quickly and skilfully.

Managing stress

There is no doubt that many students find exams stressful, so it is important to think about what you can do to try and reduce this. It is not necessarily easy and how you do this will vary from person to person. The most important thing is to find what works for you and to do it. But be aware too that a technique might work for you for a while, and you may then need to change your approach. Here are some ideas of things that might help you to reduce your stress levels during the whole exam period.

○ Time management – in Theme 9.1 we saw the importance of a workable revision plan and this in itself should help to reduce stress levels. Going back to Theme 2 to review your approach to time management could also be helpful at this point.

○ Physical exercise – this uses up our excess adrenalin and releases endorphins, or our 'feel good' hormones. It also forces us to take some time out and distracts us from whatever is making us anxious. All exercise is good, but revising can often mean we spend a lot of time indoors, and some fresh air can do a lot to revitalise us. Whatever exercise you choose to do, make sure it is something you enjoy.

○ Relaxation techniques – many of these involve breathing exercises and taking time to relax each part of your body whilst lying down and perhaps listening to some relaxing music. It is often said that 20 minutes of relaxation equates to two hours of sleep. A simple thing like relaxing in a hot bath can also be very soothing. Progressive muscle relaxation (PMR) can also be helpful for alleviating stress. This involves a sequence of steps for tightening and then relaxing groups of muscles. PMR is particularly helpful at times when stress levels are high, and because you don't need to lie down you can do it anywhere, even in the exam room.

○ Use your support networks – don't forget your study group and your friends as they will no doubt need your support too.

○ Make some time for yourself – take some time out regularly to do things you enjoy. This can be a reward for sticking to your revision plan, which can be very motivating.

- Try to avoid unhealthy habits – we can easily crave comfort food when we are feeling stressed but things like smoking, eating sugary snacks and drinking (including caffeine) can leave us feeling worse.
- Consider trying some health remedies – there are a wide range of these on the market ranging from 'rescue remedies' to herbal teas.
- Think positively – remember times when you have done well in exams and focus on these.
- Keep your eye on the end goal – this is exam time and it will not last forever.

Many universities offer special activities during exam times to help students to cope with stress, so do look out for them and take part if you feel you need to do so. There is no single way to manage stress, but only a range of things to try. Find what works for you and do more of it and be willing to share the things that work with those around you, as they could also give you more ideas. Remember it is normal to feel nervous in an exam situation. If you are too relaxed or too nervous you probably won't perform as well as you could; finding the right balance is key.

Try this

Now think about how you can manage your own stress levels during the exam period. Make a list of things you will you try and add these into your revision plan.

Activity   A detailed revision plan

Following the steps in Theme 9.1, continue making a revision plan for the exam period. Be sure to include all the relevant dates and times and your plans for taking some 'time out'. Then make a detailed plan for the coming week or fortnight, whatever works best for you.

Case study: Getting very anxious about exams

Keeleigh has always found exams very difficult and, as a result, deliberately chose a degree course with few exams. But she still has to do a number of them as part of her course and as time goes on she can feel her levels of anxiety rising as exam time approaches. She has built a good relationship with her personal tutor and finds the tutor very supportive; she decides to go and see the tutor to discuss how she is feeling.

Keeleigh takes along her revision plan to show her tutor and the tutor is interested to see how she is organising her time. The tutor says that her plan is very good but advises her to be sure to have some time off, so she can stay alert and refreshed. They also discuss the range of activities that the university has on offer to help students reduce their stress levels during the exam period. Keeleigh decides to try attending a yoga session to see if this helps reduce her levels of anxiety.

The tutor also asks Keeleigh about the things that have helped her in the past when she has become anxious, and she remembers the remedies she has used to help her relax. Keeleigh decides to take a trip to the local health food shop to buy them so she can use them when she needs to. Keeleigh also explains how taking time out and relaxing with her family has helped, and her tutor encourages her to think about planning a weekend at home in the near future, so she can relax and have a complete break from her studies.

Keeleigh leaves her tutorial feeling much more positive. In particular, she realises that she has found talking about her stress levels and getting things out of her head very helpful. She decides to make sure that she meets regularly with friends to give her more relaxation time, whilst still being determined to use her revision plan flexibly and to her benefit.

Top tip   **Think about reducing your screen time**

There is growing evidence to suggest that looking at screens (such as on your computer, TV or mobile phone) before you go to bed can affect your sleep. These screens emit a bluish light, which affects our body's natural cycles (known as circadian rhythms) that tell us when to go to sleep and when to wake up in response to light and dark. Exposure to screens during the two hours before you go to bed can affect your ability to fall asleep and can prevent you from getting a good night's rest. You can then find yourself waking up in the morning feeling tired and 'groggy' as a result. This is not a good option, particularly during your exam period.

Get into the habit of winding down and relaxing before you go to bed. Turn off all your screens and focus on something else, for example talking to friends or listening to music. You are then more likely to sleep well and to wake up feeling refreshed.

Theme 10

Personal development

This section will:

- ○ Help you think about how to build on your strengths
- ○ Encourage you to explore your weaknesses and how you might be able to overcome them
- ○ Build your resilience in the face of setbacks
- ○ Help you to think about moving on to the next level in your studies
- ○ Encourage you to start thinking about planning your future after you graduate.

> Twenty years from now you will be more disappointed by the things that you didn't do than by the ones you did do. – **Mark Twain (1835–1910) American writer, publisher and lecturer**

Building on your strengths

We are now reaching the end of the first part of the Journal, and at this point it is good to 'take stock' and review your personal and learning development. Smale and Fowlie (2009: 30) argue that 'Developing a realistic picture of who you are, is the first step in planning your personal development'. A key part of this is understanding your strengths and being clear about what you are good at. Most of us thrive when we have the opportunity to achieve our potential, and where we have the chance to grow.

Strengths can be grouped together into the following categories:

○ Skills – these are things that you can do well. This can include such things as essay writing, practical work and time management.

○ Knowledge – this includes things that you know and understand. Examples here are having an understanding of particular theories, and practical knowledge, such as knowing your way round the relevant sections of the library or student portal.

○ Attitudes or qualities – here you might think of the positive things others might say about you; for example, hard working, well-motivated, conscientious and supportive.

Being aware of your strengths will help you in the following areas:

○ Optional modules – often degree programmes include some optional modules and choosing these carefully will be important for your success. Remember too that if these are done in your second or third year (Level 5 or Level 6), your marks will 'count' towards your overall degree classification. Being aware of your academic strengths and choosing subjects you are good at means you are more likely to succeed and gain the degree classification you really want.

○ Understanding how you achieve the most – again, when it comes to optional modules, it will be good to understand which assessment methods suit you best, so you can choose your modules accordingly. Balancing your workload will be important too, so choosing a mix of modules including some asking for course work handed in during the semester and others with examinations at the end can be a good strategic approach.

○ Don't lose sight of what you enjoy – people usually achieve more doing things they enjoy and studying is no exception to this.

Looking forward, all of this will help as you begin to consider your plans for what you will do following graduation. Even though this might feel a long way ahead now, it's still worth bearing it in mind, as time has a habit of passing quickly, especially when you are enjoying what you do.

Try this   Now make a list of the things that you have enjoyed the most this year about your course, and about university life more generally.

Developing your weaker areas

We all have weaknesses, or things that we find difficult or could learn to do better. This applies to everyone, even those people who seem to be good at everything! Often it is easier to think about our areas for development rather than our weaknesses, as this is a more positive approach. Like strengths, weaknesses are all very individual, so what one person finds easy, someone else might find difficult. We need to be sure to focus on our ourselves and not on other people, so we can be clear about the areas where we need to develop, and then take appropriate action.

Here are some steps to follow to help you to think about your areas for development.

○ Face the fear – this can be difficult, as it usually means facing up to things we would rather ignore or forget. Taking the 'ostrich' approach and 'burying your head in the sand' rarely works. You might feel better in the short term, but it will soon wear off! By the time it does, you will have lost some useful development time.

○ Think about those times when you feel you haven't done very well – this means facing disappointment head on. Make sure that you have the feedback you need to improve and, if you feel you need more, remember to ask for it. When you have the feedback, be sure to read it and implement it. Unless you do this, you will probably continue to work at the same level and may even make the same mistakes again.

○ Focus on opportunities – this involves finding out about all the support mechanisms available and using them. Most universities have lots of workshops and optional sessions to help you with all kinds of things like critical reading and writing, devising a good essay plan, time management and managing stress. Using them is not a sign of weakness but of strength.

○ Think about the threats – these are things that could get in the way of your development. These can be practical, such as not having a good place to study or lack of time or money, to deeper issues like low self-esteem, lack of challenge, fear of letting others down, or 'good old-fashioned' failure.

Whatever your situation, it is good to think about how you can develop next year. University life will no longer be new; hopefully you will be living with people who you get on well with, in a positive and supportive atmosphere. Most of all be prepared to be honest with yourself and to take some action; most of us know what our weaknesses are and tackling them always takes courage and commitment. But it will be worth it in the long run.

Fostering resilience

Being resilient is important in all areas of life; without it we can become vulnerable and unable to cope. Resilience can be described as being able to 'bounce back' in the face of a setback or failure. Many students will have at least a few negative experiences while at university and having a high level of resilience will be important in order to recover, learn from the experience and carry on.

So how can you build resilience? There are two important points here. First, you need to expose yourself to risk. At university this is usually not an issue as continuing with study will automatically involve taking risks. For example, each time you submit an assignment you take some kind of risk, as it opens you up to the possibility of failure, or at least, not getting the mark you would like. This means there are many opportunities to develop resilience. However, putting yourself at risk when you have little chance of success is not to be recommended. So, for example, taking the exam without the necessary revision or submitting the essay without putting in much effort is foolish and can, if you continue to do this persistently, damage your confidence. On the other hand, we know that if we constantly 'play it safe' by doing just enough, we can feel disappointed and dissatisfied later. This is when the 'what if' questions can emerge, such as 'what if I'd put in more effort' or even 'if only I had'! So, it's all about managing risk – not too much and not too little.

Second, we all need support. We need people we can turn to when things don't go the way we want or expect. Here a good relationship with your tutors will be essential. They will be able to help you to think through what you did and how you will be able to improve. They will also be able to advise you on relevant study skills strategies that will help you to find a positive way forward. Don't forget to harness the help of family and friends too, as they will often be your greatest supporters.

Try this   Now think of a time when you experienced a setback. How did you overcome it and what might you do differently next time?

Moving on to the next level of your studies

The end of the academic year means more opportunities to consider, including looking forward to studying at a higher level next year. At this point it is well worth taking a bit of time to think through some relevant issues.

The summer vacation will be longer than you have been used to and it is definitely good to make the best of it while you can. You might want to:

○ Do some paid work to help you through the next year and to start (or continue) to build your CV for when you graduate.

○ Do some voluntary work. Even if you're not sure what you want to do after university, think about doing some work experience or a short internship, as this can help you in your decision making further down the line.

○ Travel and see parts of the world you haven't seen before. There are student discounts available and lots of opportunities for cheap fares and accommodation. You'll meet more new people and travelling is an excellent way of building your confidence, resilience and independence. You might even be able to combine this with some paid work if you're lucky.

○ Spend time with family and friends who you might not have seen for a while.

Whatever you do, be sure to get some rest and enjoy your break from studying. This means you will return to university refreshed and ready for the next academic year.

Before the end of the vacation it will be useful to prepare for the next year by doing some of the following.

○ Read through your module outlines for the coming year – this means you will start the academic year on a strong footing as you will know what to expect

○ Do some preliminary reading – this will save you valuable time later on in the term or semester

○ Look closely at the assessment criteria for the level of study above – this means you will see what the work in the coming year will demand of you

○ Start to plan – in general terms, think about what you will need to do and by when; you will be able to fill in the detail later.

The end of the academic year is a good time to reflect on what you have achieved and to set yourself some goals for next year. Academic years are notoriously short, so doing this now will help you to make the most of the time you have available.

Starting to plan for your future

Thinking about the future after graduation can be difficult and daunting for a number of reasons. Here are some of them, and you may well be able to think of more.

○ Many students decide to go to university because they don't know what they want to do in the future. This is not necessarily a bad decision, especially if you do well in your degree. On average graduates earn more than non-graduates, and university life also gives many opportunities to add valuable things to your CV through part-time, temporary or voluntary work. During your time at university you will develop some of the skills that employers are looking for; for example, a range of communication skills and team work. There will also be many intangible benefits too, such as opportunities to show commitment and grow in confidence and resilience.

○ Dealing with uncertainty is usually difficult, hence the well-known phrase 'tell me yes, tell me no, but don't tell me maybe'. Most of us like to know what is coming up next, so we can be ready for it.

○ Career can be a scary word for many people for a number of reasons. It often means making big decisions; deciding where and what to study at university involves making big decisions too, but many university students say that this 'pales into insignificance' compared to making career decisions following graduation.

○ The concept of career is abstract and here you might be tempted to think 'how will I know that's what I want to do when I haven't been able to try it?' This is where vacation work or a summer internship can be very valuable. Even if the result is knowing that this is not what you want to do after all, you will then be in a better position to decide what you do want to do in the future.

It is reassuring to know that few people make career decisions for life, as during their lifetime many people change career, and, of course, the labour market constantly changes too. However, it is a mistake to think that you can try lots of different things because this would affect your CV adversely and make you appear indecisive. If you have no idea what you want to do when you graduate, try looking at the Prospects website under 'What can I do with my degree?', click on the subject you are studying and look at the career suggestions. You could also book an appointment with someone in the careers and employability section too. Remember, the sooner you start to think about the future, the more time you will have to do all you can to put yourself in the best possible position to succeed.

Try this   Go back to the activity at the end of Theme 1 and review your vision for the future. Has this changed, and if so, how? If not, how can you be sure to continue to maintain it?

Activity   **Things to be proud of and things to work on**

Use this space to write a summary of the things you have achieved this year that you are proud of. Remember to include your academic work and things outside as well. Which areas do you now want to work on?

Case study: Wanting to do well

Afia is in the first year of her degree in Psychology. She has been progressing well but is not yet achieving the marks she would like. She has set her sights on a degree with first class honours, but most of her marks so far have been high in the 2:1 band. She goes to see one of her module tutors to discuss how she might be able to reach her goals. At the meeting the tutor points out that her work often includes errors, especially in referencing, and that she could read more widely so she will be less reliant on standard texts.

Following the meeting, Afia spends some time thinking about the points the tutor has made and makes a plan for what she will do over the summer and during the next academic year in order to improve.

○ Read more widely – she looks at next year's module reading lists and decides to borrow a small number of books from the library. She plans when she will read these over the summer.

○ Continue to work on time management – she knows that she still tends to put off assignment writing and is always in danger of running out of time when the deadline is approaching. This means she doesn't have enough time to check through her work carefully for errors. She decides to start planning her time for the first semester/term over the summer.

○ Find a good proof reader – she feels this will help her, as she knows she will not be able to see all the errors in her work herself. She decides to speak to friends and family about this.

○ Attend a workshop on referencing at the beginning of the next academic year – she realises that this is an area where she has been losing marks and that this could make a difference.

Afia is pleased that she has had the discussion with her tutor and is determined to perform to the best of her ability next year.

Top tip   **Starting to think about the future**

Many students say their time at university passes very quickly and it is good to think ahead. The idea of career can be a scary concept as it might make you think of questions like 'What am I going to do with the rest of my life?' However, for most people it is more a question of 'What am I going to do next?'

Many universities hold careers fairs and employer events to help you to begin to think things through. These give you a good opportunity to talk to people directly about what you might want to do and the sectors you might want to work in. In addition, your careers centre or employability service may well run workshops to help you to explore your strengths and interests and develop the skills needed for selection processes. They will also give you help with applying for jobs and postgraduate courses. Some student societies have links with employers too and these can be good ways of meeting people who have similar career interests and aspirations.

Part 2

Record keeping and next steps

In this section you will be able to keep a note of important information which will help you to track your progress. Keeping a record like this will help you to review your development. It is also likely to save you time in the future when you need to find things. For example, it is easy to forget where you have read something or found something that you need to draw on later and unless you have some kind of record, finding it again will probably be very time consuming.

Assessment dates

Module title	Assessment (e.g. essay)	Submission date

Marks and grades

Module title	Assessment (e.g. essay)	Mark received	Grade

Feedback received

Module title	Piece of assessed work	Development points

Useful resources

Make a note of any useful resources you have found (e.g. websites, books, articles) and where you found them.

Resource	Where found

Plans for the coming year – choosing optional modules

Make a list here of the optional modules you are thinking about and write down the pros and cons of each.

Optional module	Pros	Cons

Work experience and voluntary work

Dates	Employer	Experience gained

Plans for the summer vacation

Think about how you plan to use the next summer vacation and make some notes here.

Rest and relaxation

Travel

Paid/voluntary work

Reading

Preparing for the next academic year

Goals for the next academic year

Development point	Action	Date	Achieved

Key terms

Here is a list of key terms used by many universities that you may not have come across before. This list is not exhaustive and sometimes terms can vary depending on where you are studying.

Alumni – previous graduates of the university

APCL (Accreditation of Prior Certified Learning) – a process for recognising previous qualifications

APEL (Accreditation of Prior Experiential Learning) – a process for recognising the learning gained through previous experience

APL (Accreditation of Prior Learning) – a general term for both of the above

Appeal – the process for questioning the mark or grade given if you feel that the correct procedures haven't been applied

Bibliography – a list of sources and things you have read in relation to a piece of assessed work, but that you have not necessarily referred to

Changes to study – changing mode of study (e.g. from full-time to part-time) or to a different programme

Classification – the term used to describe the final grading system at undergraduate level

Course – sometimes used as an alternative term for module

Elective module – modules chosen from anywhere in the university (within timetable constraints)

Extenuating circumstances – things that have got in the way of being able to perform well in assessment (e.g. illness, bereavement) that allow you to apply for an extension to a work deadline

Formative assessment – assessment for feedback and development only

Interruption – permission to take a break from your studies usually because of challenging circumstances

Learning outcome – a way of describing what you will learn in each module and what you will be expected to know and understand by the end of the module

Level 0 – Foundation year

Level 4 – Year 1 of full-time undergraduate study (Years 1 and 2 of part-time study)

Level 5 – Year 2 of undergraduate study (Years 3 and 4 of part-time study)

Level 6 – Year 3 of undergraduate study (Years 5 and 6 of part-time study)

Level 7 – Masters level

Level 8 – Doctoral level

Library catalogue – an online guide to finding things you need in the library

Module tutor – the first point of contact if you need academic support

Module evaluation questionnaire – an opportunity to say what you liked and disliked about a module

Module outline – a short guide to everything involved in a module

Optional module – usually chosen from a list of prescribed modules

Personal tutor – the first point of contact if you need general support

Plagiarism – trying to pass off someone else's work as your own and a form of cheating

Portal – an online repository for lots of relevant information for students

Programme – often used instead of course

Programme handbook – a vital source of information about many aspects of your studies

References – a list of sources you have referred to in your work

Re-submission – an opportunity to re-do a piece of work if you did not get a pass grade last time.

The mark will usually be capped at the pass mark (e.g. 40%)

Special arrangements – a record of the support you will need if you have any additional needs

(e.g. dyslexia)

Staff student liaison – an important meeting for airing your views on your studies

Summative assessment – submitted work where the mark gained counts towards your overall mark

Turnitin – an online tool for submitting assessed work and checking work for plagiarism

VLE (Virtual Learning Environment) – gives online access to relevant study materials

Withdrawal – leaving university during your course with no intention of returning

References

Adams, J., Hayes, J. and Hopson, B. (1976) *Transition: Understanding and Managing Personal Change*. London: Martin Robertson.

Bedford, D. and Wilson, E. (2013) *Study Skills for Foundation Degrees*, 2nd edn. Abingdon: Routledge.

Burns, T. and Sinfield, S. (2012) *Essential Study Skills: The Complete Guide to Success at University*, 3rd edn. London: Sage.

Clarke, A. (2005) *IT Skills for Successful Study*. Basingstoke: Palgrave Macmillan.

Cottrell, S. (2013) *The Study Skills Handbook*, 4th edn. London: Red Globe Press.

Covey, S. (2004) *The 7 Habits of Highly Effective People: Restoring the Character Ethic*. New York: Free Press.

Eales-Reynolds, L-J., Judge, B., McCreery, E. and Jones, P. (2013) *Critical Thinking Skills for Education Students*, 2nd edn. London: Sage.

Honey, P. and Mumford, A. (2000) *The Learning Styles Helper's Guide*. Maidenhead: Peter Honey Publications.

Locke, E.A. and Latham, G.P. (1990) 'Work and motivation: The high performance cycle', in U. Kleinbeck, H-H. Quast and H. Hacker (eds) *Work Motivation*. Brighton: Lawrence Erlbaum Associates.

Metcalfe, M. (2006) *Reading Critically at University*. London: Sage.

Maslow, A. H. (1943) 'A theory of human motivation', *Psychological Review*, 50:4, pp. 370–396.

Pears, R. and Shields, G. (2016) *Cite Them Right*, 10th edn. London: Red Globe Press.

Smale, B. and Fowlie, J. (2009) *How to Succeed at University: An Essential Guide to Academic Skills and Personal Development*. London: Sage.

Tomlinson, M. (2017) 'Student perceptions of themselves as consumers of higher education', *British Journal of Sociology of Education*, 38:4, pp. 450–467.

Index